Read What Others Are ~~Saying About~~

Who Will Do What By When

"Working with Tom and Birgit to apply the principles discussed in *Who Will Do What By When?* has transformed our team. We have become more excited, committed and productive in our personal and professional lives."

William A. Smotherman, Director
Resource Planning - Energy Supply
Tampa Electric Company

"This book will be show cased along side other best sellers *One Minute Manger* and *Who Moved My Cheese* as a fulfilling read with a high-impact story. I was totally captivated by this powerful book."

Peggy McColl
Author of *On Being a Dog with a Bone*
www.destinies.com

"I loved reading this book. It describes a great way to live — a hard way, but a great way. If you really follow this I can guarantee your life and performance will be better, but don't buy it if you aren't prepared to change."

Sam Ginzburg, Senior Trader, Partner
First New York Securities

"This book is fantastic. After reading more than half of it before trying to go to sleep, I couldn't stop thinking about the basic team building principles Coach was teaching Jake so I got back up and finished the entire book. Great characters and easy and delightful reading."

Keith Guevara, CEO
NBO Systems, Inc.

"The book energized me. I've read tons of leadership books in my life and I'd rank this among the best. I can put that chart right in front of me and use it to guide me through any interpersonal challenges I have. And it's not just a leadership book; as a leader you'd want your players to read it, it will put you all in the same mindset. I would have called it 'How to Be a Team Leader and Team Player.'"

John Otterness, CEO
Otterness Construction Company

"I found the book to be the best guide to being a good manager and a good person that I have come across. I am going to request that my group of managers read and share it with their supervisors!"

Paul Ziegler, VP, Central Pinellas Market Manager
First National Bank

"A must read book. In addition to the invaluable team productivity principles it teaches, the book provides an example of the power of coaching. The process has changed my life and my sense of responsibility."

Tom Trexler, CEO
Corporate Finance Institute

"Before we started working with Tom and Birgit we were experiencing considerable inefficiency and tension amongst our staff. Since the *Who Will Do What By When* workshops and coaching we're at a much higher level of performance – and my stress level is way down. I recommend this program to anyone who wants to upgrade their organization's performance."

Julian Garcia, Director
University Area Community Development Complex
Tampa

"This book communicates in a clear and precise manner how every leader can sustain, motivate, and inspire. I found the book a 'must read' for those wishing to get to and stay at the top."

Dr. Ben Lerner
N.Y. Times Best Selling Author of *Body By God*

"The Integrity Tools outlined are not only a guide to good business; they apply to every aspect of your life as well. Your system is easy to understand, share and use."

Delores Kesler, Former Chairman and CEO
AccuStaff (now MPS Group)

"We all know that there have been many books written about performance, communication and leading a positive life. This is one of the few that combines these important topics concisely and presents the lessons in an engaging and entertaining style. I'm excited to start improving how I interact and communicate with my teammates and my clients."

Mark Segel, CFP, Vice President/Commercial Lender
The Bank of Tampa

"The book effectively illustrates how great business and personal goals can be achieved through integrity... an often overlooked element in today's society."

Bill Bardwell, CEO
Biometric Security Company

"Before working with Heads-Up Performance we weren't capitalizing on all of the opportunities we knew were out there. They helped us implement systems that brought our performance results up sharply and our stress levels down significantly. They really made a dramatic difference."

Scott Jaffe
Senior Vice President, Smith-Barney

"The potential and power of the human brain is enormous. Tom and Birgit's book successfully guides the reader - with an engaging storyline - toward tapping into that power by providing the "how-tos" of business integrity."
Doug Bench, M.S., J.D.
Science For Success Systems
www.ScienceForSuccess.com

"Birgit and Tom have the expertise to walk their talk."
Sandy Crowe, Authority on Dealing with Difficult People
Author of *Since Strangeling Isn't An Option*

"As the owner of a business devoted to helping other businesses develop superior sales cultures, I've had the occasion to read a lot of business books over the years. While most have something to recommend in them, few provide insights with such immediate applicability as *Who Will Do What By When?* It addresses real business and human interaction issues and does so in an entertaining format. I like to get a good return on my reading time investment; this book delivered beyond expectations."
Mark Fitzgerald, Owner
Sales Training Institute, Inc.

"Birgit and Tom's book is a must read for anyone who needs to get a team to perform. It outlines a simple, practical strategy for clear communication and follow-through."
Leigh Ann Haller, President
Haller Industries, Inc.

"Terrific! The book brings a new definition to the power integrity carries in the workplace. Something as seemingly harmless as being continuously late for meetings carries a big price in terms of how you are perceived in the office or at home and results in integrity depletion. I recommend this book as a key tool in your personal integrity management toolbox!"

Bill Hearl, Ph.D., Chief Scientific Officer
Capital Genomix, Inc.

"In an era where corporations have become synonymous with a lack of integrity, this book provides a welcome solution. It is a proven approach to building accountability, trust, and personal power."

Dennis L. Rasmussen, Retired MLB Pitcher
Wealth Advisory Specialist, Legg Mason

"This is a wonderful guide for building a strong foundation in business. We know our integrity is a fundamental reason for our success, and we're happy to be Jake and Christine's favorite restaurant - they're welcome anytime!"

Dory Abi-najm, Owner
The Lebenese Taverna

Who Will Do What By When?

How To Improve Performance, Accountability And Trust With Integrity

Tom Hanson, Ph.D.
Birgit Zacher Hanson, M.S.

POWER
Publications, Inc.

Dedication

To Christopher J. Hanson
Our Favorite "Who"

Table Of Contents

Introduction

*Your personal reputation and the success of your
organization depend on your ability to make
and fulfill promises.*

Mention integrity in the business world today and
Enron, Tyco and other multi-million dollar criminal wrong-
doings come to mind. But millions of dollars are lost daily
in acts that don't make the newspapers, mainly because they
aren't crimes.

It isn't a crime if you say you will complete a report by
2 p.m. Friday, and you don't do it; nor is it a crime if a boss
makes her staff wait 20 minutes before showing up at a
meeting. But in each case a multi-layered cost is paid by all
involved.

Your word is your most important business asset.
Leaders say they want their people to operate with integrity,
but few operationally define it or have a clearly defined
system they teach to improve it. According to business guru
W. Edwards Deming, 94% of failures result from not
adhering to an effective system.

In the following story we introduce an effective system
for operating with integrity. Drawing from the work of
many of our teachers and coaches (see *Book Content*

Acknowledgements at the end of the book), the system is a series of familiar actions, such as *request, promise* and *acknowledgement,* applied in a more rigorous, clearly defined way. We call the actions Integrity Tools because they help build, maintain and restore integrity to any interpersonal situation.

Just like your computer, your work team has an operating system (a pattern of norms and practices usually not expressed formally) which governs interactions between team members. The power of your operating system determines the reliability, speed, and bandwidth of your team's performance. Installing the system we offer here upgrades your team's "interpersonal" operating system.

Creating a culture of integrity and accountability not only improves effectiveness, it also generates a respectful, enjoyable and life-giving setting in which to work. This is a welcome alternative to the typical suffocating environment where employees feel forced to choose between their own values and success at work.

We focus on integrity not because it is our favorite subject, but because it is the foundation of interpersonal excellence, and most teams and individuals we coach are unaware of its power and how to capture it. As a result they suffer needlessly. Returning to the computer analogy, if the operating system is faulty, none of our other programs can run effectively.

We hope that you also see the value of these ideas beyond the business world. The same tools enhance performance, accountability, and trust in all areas of life including family, friendships, sports teams, and, as we see in this story, love.

Finally, although the ideas in the system may seem simple, they usually are not easy to apply. But rest assured, if you only remember to say the title of this book several minutes before the end of your meetings, the book will have been a great investment!

Prologue

It was opening day of the Major League Baseball season and Jake wanted to be home watching the line-up of games on ESPN. Instead, he was having another bad day at work. He had no idea that for him, today would be an *opening day* of a different sort.

PART ONE

❖

Opening Day

Jake Blows Up

Jake was late for his Wednesday staff meeting, but that's not what infuriated him. The file he promised to send to a customer two hours ago was stuck somewhere in cyberspace. Although *his* error had created the problem, Jake cursed and blamed his computer's newly upgraded operating system.

Ten stressful minutes later he stormed into the conference room with lightning in his eyes and a vice-tight jaw. Frustration spun his mind too fast for him to notice the dirty looks he got from his five-person staff. They'd been waiting for nearly 20 minutes — and this wasn't the first time.

"You people are driving me nuts," Jake began sternly. "I just don't understand why you aren't producing. Last week's numbers just came in, and once again you are all well below your quotas. I just don't get it, what is going on?"

No one knew if he expected an answer, but they weren't going to risk giving him one. Instead, they boarded up their emotional windows and braced themselves: Hurricane Jake had just come ashore.

In his mid-thirties, Jake McKay had the kind of athletic frame men respected and women eyed. He stood tall (a bit over six-feet-one-inch) and still had all of his signature wavy black hair. But his look was changing: his face was a bit fuller, his cheeks a bit redder, and his clothes a bit tighter than just a few months ago. His buddies now teased him about getting a "manager's body."

Jake's dark good looks had always helped him close sales. A gifted athlete, his dream of playing professional baseball was snuffed out by a knee injury in college. A family friend introduced him to the insurance business and it was a perfect match for his abilities and goals. With ten years of successful sales under his belt, he had recently been named Washington, D.C. district sales manager of Freedom Mutual Insurance Company. He had never been in a management position before and he wanted to stay. But reflecting on the first four months in his new position, he wondered how that would be possible.

The team's insurance sales had floundered since Jake took the helm, and the total office sales figures were in the bottom 40 percent of all district offices nationally for Freedom Mutual. Jake had tried to be patient, but he wasn't used to losing, and today a storm surge of emotion erupted.

"Bill," spewed Jake, addressing the 53-year-old, silver-haired veteran sitting with rounded shoulders to Jake's right, "you're my senior sales rep. You used to be a top performer. Now you're on cruise control going half speed. You should be leading this team—setting the example. Actually, I take that back. You *are* setting an example—a poor one. Keep in mind you still have a long way to go to retirement, unless you want it to come early."

The other four staff members winced in unison at that comment and nervously waited for their turn in Jake's path.

"And Tad," Jake rolled on, "I really don't get you. You have everything going for you – you look like a million bucks in your fancy clothes, but you produce more like a two dollar bill."

Except for his solemn face, Tad did look good. He was an affable, young thirty-something fashion plate who wore Gucci loafers and Armani suits. He really looked the part of the successful insurance sales rep, but he worked off other people and took credit for their sales whenever possible. Why he didn't just forge ahead and create more sales by himself was more than Jake (or anyone else) could figure out.

"Jean," sighed Jake as the gale continued, "Jean, Jean, Jean. I can't tell you what I want to tell you because I'm afraid you'll start to cry. When I was in your position I just did what I had to do, and I have a hard time understanding why you can't do the same."

Her colleagues called her Drama Queen Jean. She knew her stuff well enough, but her two teenage boys kept her hopping, and she complained about one personal crisis after another. Lately she had been taking everything Jake said too personally, always getting emotional and upset.

5

Jake wanted to help her, but didn't know how to handle a 45-year-old woman who acted like a child! True to form, she was fighting back tears now, so Jake moved on.

"Nathan," said Jake, "you have the lowest numbers on the team. I really don't know what to do with you, and to be honest, I don't expect a whole lot more, but I would appreciate it if you would surprise me sometime."

Everyone knew Nathan landed this job through a family connection to the C.E.O. of Freedom Mutual. Everyone also knew the skinny, geek of a young man had no aptitude or enthusiasm for the insurance business, but because of his political connections no one would discuss this topic. Nathan sort of coasted along on his shy but pleasant personality, and people usually didn't mind picking up the slack for him.

"Crystal," Jake said to the tightly wound intellectual woman in her late-twenties. "You are the only one really performing anywhere near your potential; but even you can do better, especially if you would learn to work *with* instead of *against* the other people in this room. If I had you as a student, I would write 'doesn't play well with others' on your report card."

Jake paused, took a deep breath and exhaled through pursed lips. The staff wondered if the storm was over, or if this was the eye of the storm and more destruction would follow.

During the calm, the thought crept into Jake's head that he was being an ass. It wasn't like him to thrash people like this, but he was at a loss for what else to do.

"Listen people," he finally said, "I'm in no mood to even talk this through with you right now so I'm just going to let you go. Use what's left of the afternoon to think about what I've said here today. I know you are all capable of so much more. I've tried being nice to you so far, and now I need to hold your feet to the fire. If you're having trouble with something in particular, stay and talk to me, otherwise I'll see you tomorrow."

Although their heads were filled with sharp comebacks, Bill, Tad, Jean, Nathan and Crystal all shuffled out of the room without saying a word. None of them had escaped unscathed, and they were all smart enough to know this was not the time to discuss anything with Jake.

Aftermath

Jake pushed himself back from the head of the 20-foot cherry wood conference table, loosened his tie and slumped deep into his red leather chair. He wistfully looked around the beautiful conference room with its expensive artwork, luxurious spruce green oriental carpet, and tasteful brass decorative accessories.

He loved this room – so many of his sales triumphs had been announced here. Now it felt like a crime scene. Things had changed: instead of the highly successful salesman, he was now the lowly unsuccessful manager.

His thoughts shifted from his underperforming team to his underperforming self. Not only had his circumstances changed, *he* had changed too. Jake had always thought of himself as a good guy, enjoyable to be around, caring and respectful. But the stress of his new position had morphed him into an insensitive, disrespectful guy who had just embarrassed his colleagues in front of each other. He felt as if he were starring in an episode of *The Incredible Hulk*: *Mild-Mannered Man Becomes Violent Tempest.*

Good grief, he thought as he reflected on the meeting. *What did I just do? What is going on with me? I'm becoming the manager I always disliked when I was a rep.*

9

Is there something about becoming a manager that makes a guy go stupid?

Jake's thoughts quickly turned to the events of three days earlier. It would be a long time before he forgot the quiet warning Chuck Helfer delivered to him as he was preparing to leave the home office in Belton, New Jersey. That one sentence still rang in his ears, "If you don't pull your team out of this slump and get your figures up where they belong, I'm not sure we can justify keeping you in management."

Jake understood that as senior vice president of sales, Chuck had no choice in making the situation clear to him. He had done it kindly, although firmly. Chuck had always supported him. Jake knew that he would never have been promoted to district sales manager without Chuck's endorsement.

He couldn't let Chuck down! He couldn't let himself down, either. For that matter, he couldn't let his team down by letting them get away with this dismal performance. Somehow he had to whip them into shape, help them get their enthusiasm back, and get them to work together, but how? How could he fight an enemy he couldn't even define?

The one thing he did *not* want was to go back to being a sales representative, although he was very good at it. That would be a step backwards on his career path, and he didn't think other people, especially his girlfriend, Christine, would understand that.

Christine, Jake said to himself. The thought of her gave him a moment's reprieve, *at least one thing in my life is going well.*

A senior nurse at Georgetown University Hospital, Christine was right where she wanted to be and she had worked hard to get there. Jake admired her so much! Actually, it was more than that. He loved her. He knew she wanted to get married and start a family, but he just couldn't think about that right now. He had to straighten out this mess at work, and he had to do it pronto. He knew something was fundamentally wrong, but he had no idea what it was.

This year Freedom Mutual was doing something special for its top producing offices. Instead of taking only its top performing representatives and managers to the national sales convention in New York, *every* member of each office that finished in the top ten percent gets to go. But Jake's original goal of having his whole team qualify for the trip now seemed like a joke.

Jake had been able to attend the convention for the past eight years as a top sales representative for Freedom Mutual. He knew this event was a Big League way of saying thank you and wanted his team to experience the satisfaction and fun that came with it.

Jake had a plan for getting this group there, but they weren't helping. Jake had told them numerous times that they needed to set at least ten new appointments a week to get enough new people into the pipeline, but they kept falling short – a team-wide sales slump. It seemed as though they didn't even care about their own paycheck, not to mention the team's overall figures. He was tired of hearing their excuses.

But now what? The staff looked pretty beaten as they left today's meeting. Who could blame them? Although berating them felt good to Jake at the time, it was clearly not the right approach.

Discouraged, Jake stood up, grabbed his jacket from the back of his chair, collected his files, and headed out of the conference room. He was meeting Christine for dinner later, but needed to make one stop first.

Since becoming a manager, Jake had wanted to talk with his old baseball coach and get some pointers on leadership. Twice before today Jake had promised Coach he would stop by the Little League field where Coach managed a summer team, and twice Jake had cancelled. Although he felt more like going home and cracking open a cold beer, it would be too much to blow Coach off three times.

What You See Is What You Get

Traffic was mercifully light driving past the Jefferson Memorial and down the George Washington Parkway toward Alexandria, sparing Jake further angst and speeding his trip to the baseball complex. The Little League field was adjacent to the high school field he'd starred on years ago, so just being there made him feel a bit better. He smiled at the sight of Coach Peters teaching a little redheaded kid with glasses how to hold the bat.

Jake made his way around the neatly manicured field to the dugout and sat down. With his elbows on his knees and his hands clasped in front of him, he watched Coach work with the nine- and ten-year-olds. They seemed like a motley crew with little organization. Of course, it was only April and they had just begun practicing a week before. Coach still had time to work his magic and pull these players together as a team. *Wish I could say the same about the situation at work,* Jake thought.

Jake looked out at Coach with admiring eyes. Still in great shape at 68-years-old, Coach seemed a mix between a young and old man. A lean six-footer with physical strength much greater than met the eye, Coach's sharply lined face suggested a life of trying times and a career spent mostly outdoors. He had spring in his step, but stiffness in his shoulders.

Jake listened as Coach gave the Little Leaguers a pep talk on his number one topic: fundamentals. "Execute the fundamentals," he said, "and the winning takes care of itself."

> *Execute the fundamentals, and the winning takes care of itself.*

Coach had always been sort of an anomaly. It was obvious he loved coaching, being outside and working with the kids, but few knew he was actually an astute businessman. He believed in life-long learning and was the most well-read man Jake knew. Unbeknownst to Jake, Coach even coached business executives from time to time.

Practice ended and Coach sent the kids to their waiting moms and dads. As he made his way to the dugout, Jake stood up to greet him.

"Well, look who's here!" Coach enthusiastically pumped Jake's hand and thumped him on the shoulder. "Great to see you, Jake! How's it going?"

Jake hesitated one beat too long with his answer and Coach picked up on it, just as he always used to. That one bushy eyebrow went down and he looked into Jake's eyes just long enough to know all was not well with his friend and former all-state ballplayer.

"It's going, Coach," Jake replied with a lame attempt to sound happy.

"Sit with me for a minute, Jake," Coach said.

Will Peters had retired three years ago after an illustrious career as coach and teacher at Alexandria High. Since then he had spent his summers coaching Little League. He was a great coach and a great person everyone, including opposing coaches, admired.

Coach had a sense of peace and calmness about him, the kind that comes from having lived life authentically. Coach had been a special friend to Jake throughout his four years of high school, as well as an encouraging advisor during his college ball-playing days. Jake trusted him implicitly.

"I've got a huge problem, Coach, and I don't know how to solve it because I don't know what the real problem behind the problem really is!" Then Jake added, "Good thing you weren't my English teacher, huh?"

Coach laughed and said, "Good thing for both of us! What's going on?"

"Well," said Jake hesitantly, trying to figure out the answer to that question himself. "I'm heading up a team of insurance agents, and sales have been going down since I took over. My boss basically threatened me saying I'd better get them going or else he'd need to do some 're-organizing.' My people are slacking off and are unmotivated.

15

They're lazy and just don't care about what results they produce."

Jake paced back and forth as he told Coach a little about each of his staff members, what he had said at today's meeting, and the general status of his stressful life. The only bright spot he mentioned was Christine. Coach interrupted only to ask for clarification on a few points. When he exhausted his story, Jake expressed his hope that Coach could help him somehow and sat back down on the dugout bench.

"Wow," said Coach, "that's quite a load you're carrying. Then he asked again, "How do you think I could help you?"

"I could use some coaching! I know you coach baseball, but you were so good with our team and are so smart that I'm confident you could help me with my team."

Coach lowered that same bushy eyebrow. "I've got some great tools I enjoy teaching that are so fundamental they improve team performance on the field, in the business arena, and everywhere else. If you are willing to make a commitment, I could help you learn them."

"Great," said Jake gratefully. "I knew it would be a good idea to talk to you. I just wish I'd done it before I dug such a big hole at work. But I couldn't ask you to coach me for free."

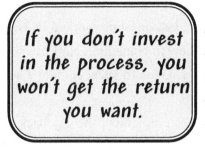

If you don't invest in the process, you won't get the return you want.

"That's part of the commitment," smiled Coach. "If you don't invest in the process you won't get the return you want."

"Coach," said Jake, "I know I could go back to being a successful salesman, but I want to move forward. I've never failed at anything, but this managing thing is kicking my butt. I would love another chance to have you coach me. What would it take to make that happen?"

After a brief conversation, the two agreed on a cash-plus-batting practice deal: Since coach's arm wasn't what it used to be, Jake would work off a small part of Coach's fee by throwing batting practice to the team once a week.

"Okay then, let's go," said Coach. "You mentioned that your staff is lazy and don't care about the results they produce, is that true?"

"For sure," said Jake, slipping easily back into complaining mode. "They have some talent, but they don't perform. They don't put in the effort. They're just there to do the bare minimum and get their paychecks, nothing more."

"Do you know for a fact that's true?" asked Coach patiently.

"Yes," Jake responded, "why they..." Jake's momentum stalled as Coach's last question worked its way through his head. "I may be new to managing, but I can sell insurance, and I know what it takes to succeed, and I see they just don't have it."

"Jake," said Coach, "do you remember the day back in high school when you and your buddy, C.J., showed up at practice with your new Oakley sunglasses?"

"Of course," said Jake, more than willing to change the subject to a happy memory. "I thought I was pretty cool. Actually, I *was* pretty cool."

"When you looked through those yellow lenses," Coach advanced, "what color was the grass?"

"Well, it looked yellow."

"That's right. How about after you'd had them on for a couple of hours, how did the grass seem to you then?"

"Normal, I guess. I got used to the lenses and forgot I had them on, so I didn't think about it."

"So was the grass being yellow a fact, which is something collectively agreed upon, or fiction, meaning

FACT
Something collectively agreed upon.

FICTION
Something made up... your interpretation.

something you made up – your interpretation?" Coach asked.

"By that definition, fiction," Jake said.

"The fact is that the grass was green," continued Coach, "but it appeared as yellow to you because you saw it through yellow lenses. If you completely forgot you had those lenses on, you would argue pretty strongly with anyone who said the grass was green."

"Yes," said Jake, ready to see where this was leading.

"We all have lenses on that color the way we see the world," said Coach. "It's just that the lenses I'm talking about are *behind* your eyes, not in front of them like your Oakleys. It's called your **perspective**. The problem with perspective is that you forget it's there. You think you see the world as it is, that what you see is the truth, but actually you see things through your own personal lenses or filters."

> ## PERSPECTIVE
> Seeing the world through your own lenses or filters.

"So you're saying the opinions I have about my staff are fiction, something I made up?" said Jake, connecting the dots.

"That's my perception," smiled Coach.

Jake sat back, considering Coach's idea.

"But before we get into that," said Coach, "let me add one more key piece. People act consistently with what they see. For example, this year I seem to have all the kids on my team no other coach wanted: the marginally talented, the under-performers, and the troublemakers. But if I see them as a bunch of unmotivated losers who would be lucky to win one game this season, how do you think I will treat them?"

"You'd probably just focus on keeping them out of trouble and not expect much of them baseball-wise," said Jake.

"Does that sound like good coaching, the kind that makes them better people and better players?"

"No."

"And do you think I would feel good about myself at the end of the season?" asked Coach.

"No," said Jake, the pieces coming together in his mind.

"Is this team capable of having a winning season?" Coach posed. "I don't know, maybe not. But one thing I do know is that I am not going to be the one that limits them by treating them like a bunch of losers. Despite how they look at first glance, I choose to see them as capable of great things, and I will coach them as if I knew they were champions. Does that guarantee that they will be? Of course not, but I know that gives them their best chance to find out how good they can be and how much fun they can have. It also is the only way I can feel good about myself when all is said and done."

"And so if I see my staff as lazy and poor performers," concluded Jake, "I'll treat them that way, and they'll perform that way. But if I see them as having the possibility of performing great...."

Jake shifted his pensive gaze from the dugout floor to the beautiful green grass of the ball field. He could feel his spirits beginning to lift.

Coach broke the silence, "As I told you, I've got some great tools I can share with you that can help your team be more effective, accountable, and trusting, as well as create a great sense of personal satisfaction."

"Let me guess? They're fundamentals," said Jake.

"Of course," said Coach. "But if you see your staff as a bunch of lazy losers, there's no point in your learning these tools. In fact, you'd probably misuse them. A hammer can be used to build or destroy a beautiful home. Before we work on the tools, we need to work on the tool user."

Coach's point made sense to Jake, though he would have preferred his staff needing to change, not himself.

"The final point I'll make about perspective," said Coach, "is that you get to choose it. Just like your Oakleys have different color lenses you can choose for them, you can choose the nature of the lenses behind your eyes. But as you know, Oakley lenses are expensive … you need to pay a fair bit for them."

"Yes, my mom wasn't too happy when I forgot them in the dugout after the McClean game and never saw them again," said Jake wistfully.

"It's pretty easy to choose a different perspective for a moment, but you have to pay a price to keep your new attitude. You have to be conscious of it, practice it, and strengthen it over time just like any skill you might learn on the baseball diamond. And this isn't just about your performance at work, Jake. Your perspective on life determines the quality of your life."

> *Your perspective on life determines the quality of your life.*

"What perspective should I choose?" asked Jake.

"Whichever one gives you the most power in a situation," said Coach. "For starters, though, you need to choose between being a **victim**, who focuses on how hard the challenge is and how difficult external circumstances are making it to succeed, and being a **player**, who focuses on what he can do to create success. A player plays the game; a victim lets the game play him. Which do you think you're being in regard to your staff?"

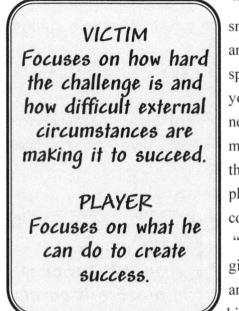

VICTIM
Focuses on how hard the challenge is and how difficult external circumstances are making it to succeed.

PLAYER
Focuses on what he can do to create success.

"I hear you, Coach," smiled Jake, the answer too obvious to speak. "Sounds like you're prescribing a new set of lenses for me. I'm happy to have the chance to be a player with you as my coach again."

"One of the greatest gifts you can give anyone is to believe in him or her," Coach rolled on, beginning the end of the conversation. "We can't know what your team is capable of until you, their leader, see them as being capable of great

One of the greatest gifts you can give anyone is to believe in him or her.

things. Maybe you don't know what's going on with them. You might be interpreting behavior as laziness or incompetence when in reality something else is interfering with their performance. Keep in mind that every time you judge them, you deprive them of the opportunity to change. You set them up to become just the way you see them. That's not going to get you what you want. It will actually create the opposite."

"I guess I can see that," said Jake. "So it's sort of like, *What I see is what I get.*"

"Good one," acknowledged Coach. "Yes, your perception is a self-fulfilling prophecy. Here's your first homework assignment."

"Homework?" groaned Jake.

"You can gain insight in a conversation," Coach responded, "but the only way to change behavior is to practice on the field. Talking about it in the dugout doesn't do the trick."

> **The only way to change behavior is to practice it on the field. Talking about it in the dugout doesn't do the trick.**

"Okay," said Jake. "I suppose I should get a notebook?"

"You read my mind," said Coach. "And here's the first thing I'd like you to write about. For the next few days at the office, ask yourself if what you see is fact or fiction. Don't try to see people differently than you do now, just be aware that you look at them through your lenses, and be open to the possibility that your thoughts and perceptions are not the truth. You might even check the accuracy of some of your perceptions by asking your staff. I don't know what you'll notice, but for all we know your people might be superstars in disguise just like my Little League team."

Jake laughed at that thought and stood up. "Thanks Coach. I'll give it a try."

"Trying isn't good enough, Jake. Will you do it?"

"Sure. It certainly can't make things worse than they are."

"How will I know you did it?" Coach asked.

"I suppose I could give you a call and report back."

"That would be great. When will you call?"

"Maybe Tuesday," Jake replied, taken aback slightly by Coach's rigor.

"Maybe?" Coach asked back with a skeptical expression on his face.

"Well, no, I'll call you on Tuesday for sure."

"What time?"

"Two o'clock," Jake fired back, now smiling at the exchange.

"All right then. And I encourage you to write this homework on one of those yellow stickies and place it where you can see it. Otherwise you might forget."

Jake thanked his old coach and began the walk across the ball field to his car. Thanks to a new sense of possibility, his step had the bounce it had back in his playing days. He thought, *Was there something I didn't see in my staff? Maybe I can turn things around.*

His positive feelings lasted about 30 seconds. They ended abruptly when he looked at his watch and realized he was already 15 minutes late for dinner with Christine.

Jake Has Christine's Perspective For Dinner

As Jake raced his Jeep Cherokee through traffic on Connecticut Avenue, his mind sped through the myriad problems he was having at work. He wondered why it seemed nothing in his present life really worked very well.

Thirty-five minutes late, he parked in the underground garage and hustled toward *The Lebanese Taverna*, his and Christine's favorite restaurant. He was sure Christine had already been seated and hoped she hadn't been waiting too long. Panting as he reached the front door, he straightened his jacket and tie, and tried to compose himself before stepping inside.

He swung the heavy glass door open, made his way past the crowd at the bar, and saw Christine wave to him from their favorite table. She looked beautiful sitting there with her long dark hair flowing below her shoulders. Something special about her (beyond just her vibrant eyes and Hollywood smile) made Jake relax every time he was in her presence. At least now he felt he could unwind and enjoy a quiet evening.

Jake approached the table, leaned over and softly kissed Christine's cheek. "Sorry I'm so late," he apologized.

Christine gave him a quick smile and took a sip of her Chardonnay. As Jake sat down, he thought to himself, *I'm so lucky. I have everything I ever wanted in a relationship, and we're so happy and good together.*

"Jake," Christine's voice was shaking. "I'm not sure we should see each other any more."

Her words punched Jake in the gut. His mind was racing, but he lacked the oxygen needed to speak.

Christine continued, "We've been dating now for close to two years and even though I love you, I don't know if we want the same things in life. I'm 32, and I'm ready to settle down and have a family, but I really have no idea what you want, and, quite frankly, couldn't trust you if you told me."

Jake's brain started spinning. *What did she mean she had no idea what he wanted? How could she not know he was in love with her and wanted the same things she did? Why can't she trust me?*

"I'm not sure our relationship has a future," Christine said, emotion building inside her. "If we're going to continue as a couple, I need to know that we have a future, because right now I just don't see it."

How could each of them see the same relationship so differently? He loved her and

> **How could each of them see the same relationship so differently?**

he thought she should know that by now. Jake looked into her dark brown eyes, "I thought you knew how I felt about you, Chris."

"How would I know, Jake?" she replied, "Have you ever told me?"

Jake looked down at the empty place setting in front of him and folded his hands on the table. *Sure I have*, he thought to himself.

Or had he? Maybe he had never actually come right out and said "I love you and I want to marry you and start a family with you," but that's what he wanted. He couldn't fathom how different their perspectives were.

But the day's events had left Jake totally drained and he didn't want to have an argument in front of everyone in the restaurant, so he said, "Chris, I've just had a really bad day at work. Our sales are sinking like the *Titanic,* and everyone in the office is upset. Bill doesn't want to work any more; Tad can't get a client on his own; and Jean is a basket case who cries every time I speak to her. I really have to focus on work right now. Can we just talk about us later?"

Christine's sadness and frustration turned to anger. She stood up, threw her pocketbook strap over her shoulder, looked Jake in the eye and said, "When, Jake? By when will you be ready to have that conversation?"

When Jake balked, Christine turned away, then turned back to punctuate her charge: "And has it ever occurred to you that the people you work with are not all failures? It seems you are so busy judging them you don't even know what's going on in their lives. Do you even care?"

Although she could have gone on, she felt she had said enough, turned, and walked out of the restaurant.

Jake was left to dine with his thoughts, and they did not make pleasant company. The day's events flooded his mind: the staff meeting (or more accurately, staff *beating*) left them devastated and him lost, then the conversation with Coach that had him feeling optimistic, and now dinner with Christine had blown up. What a roller coaster! *What is going on? And what did Christine mean when she asked me if I even cared about my people?*

Jake thought back to Coach's comments about the Oakleys. *That's it!* he thought, *my staff and Christine aren't seeing things for what they are. They're viewing things through the wrong color lenses. I need to figure out how I can get them to change their perspective so they see more clearly.*

Then the same thought did a one-eighty and hit Jake like a fastball in the head. *Could it possibly be my own perceptions that are not accurate? Maybe I'm judging people too quickly. Could it be that I don't care about what's going on in their lives? Maybe I'm the one who needs to change?*

PART TWO

❖

Integrity

Fact Or Fiction?

Jake sat at his desk the next morning tapping his pen on the glass tabletop. The dark circles under his eyes testified to his sleepless night of tossing and turning. As Coach had suggested, he wrote his assignment on a yellow sticky note and stuck it to his computer monitor.

His world consisted of his sales team and Christine, and right now both had two strikes on him.

Christine didn't answer her phone when he called her last night, and now with sweaty hands and a thumping in his chest, he once again dialed her number. When her voicemail responded, it was actually a relief. He didn't know what to say anyway. He fumbled through another apology and asked her to call him. As he hung up the phone, he worried she might never speak to him again.

Jake laid his head on his desk. In a moment he dozed off and started dreaming about his high school baseball days. For some reason, he was transported to the day Clark Kamin moved to town from Stoughton, Wisconsin, and showed up for baseball practice. Clark was lanky and scrawny, wore thick glasses and had horrible acne. The consummate dork, Clark was a wise-cracker's delight. The team started in on him before Coach got there.

"What planet is that guy from?" one player quipped, getting the laughs started. "Ya, isn't it time to return to the mother ship?" trumped another. Surely Coach wasn't serious about letting this kid join the team. Clark leaned meekly against the outside wall of the dugout with his head hanging low from his goose-like neck, stirring the dirt with his size 13½ feet, absorbing the blows. The verbal onslaught continued until Coach showed up. No one was ready for what happened next.

"This is Clark Kamin, and he's going to be playing with us from now on," Coach said as the players snickered and groaned. Coach's bushy eyebrow went down and his face brightened as if he had a secret he couldn't wait to tell. He started practice without further comment. The jokes behind Clark's back continued through warm ups and fundamentals, and then it was time for batting practice.

The first few hitters passed without incident, but as Jake picked up his bat and walked to home plate to hit, Coach tapped Clark on the behind and motioned for him to head to the pitching mound. Clark jogged slowly, clumsily to the mound, put his right foot on the rubber and looked for a sign from Paul, the catcher.

"This ought to be a good laugh," the players winked to each other.

Jake looked back at Paul and said, "We'll show him how we play ball in the Capital District!" Paul pulled his mask down over his face, squatted, and held his glove out to give the new kid a target as Jake stepped up to the plate. Clark went into an awkward movement and hurled the ball in Jake's direction. The ball looked like an aspirin tablet as it whizzed past him and popped in Paul's mitt.

"Strike one," said Coach through the stunned silence.

Clark threw pitch after pitch that day, and player after player tried to hit one, yet no one did except for one foul ball. Despite his gawky frame and dorky appearance, Clark was like Superman throwing a baseball. Everyone had the wrong perception of Clark.

A distant phone ringing woke Jake and pulled him back to the present. I *wonder who I underestimate in this office?*

he thought to himself as he remembered his dream. Then he heard a knock on his door.

Bill peered in. "You okay, Jake?" The wrinkles around Bill's blue eyes and clean-shaven face deepened as he smiled in concern about Jake's groggy appearance.

"Yeah, definitely," said Jake pulling himself together. "Well, actually…. Got a minute, Bill? I think we should talk."

Jake rubbed his eyes as Bill hesitantly pulled up a dark green leather armchair and sat down across the desk from Jake. Bill sat quietly; dreading what was coming next.

Jake knew his criticism and tongue-lashing had cut his senior sales rep at yesterday's staff meeting. Jake had strong negative opinions about Bill and his performance lately, but was now willing to question if his assessments were correct or not.

Jake cleared his throat and said, "I'm not sure exactly where to start."

Apprehension on his face, Bill leaned back in his chair and crossed his arms. He was ready to take whatever Jake threw at him.

"Bill, you're the best man I have here. You have the most experience and knowledge, you have the best track record, and you know this business inside and out. I need your help."

Bill was surprised by that last line and ran his hand over his mouth to cover his reaction. "I'm at your service," he offered. "What can I do to help?"

"I've noticed a change in you the past few months, and I am not sure how to interpret it. May I ask you a question straight up?"

"Sure, fire away."

"Are you just putting in your time for retirement, or are you ...? "

Bill jolted forward with a look of disbelief on his face and interrupted Jake. "Hold it right there, Jake. I may not be the spitfire that I used to be, but I have a loyal bunch of clients who still like dealing with this old dinosaur. My ticker has slowed me down a bit, but the doc said I can start resuming my normal pace of activities now."

Bill had a heart condition? Confused, Jake buried his head in his hands, thought for a moment and then started laughing, "I'm throwing away my Oakleys, Coach!"

Jake explained the Oakley reference and even told Bill the Clark Kamin story, then pushed ahead. "I need to know what's really going on in this office. I have to learn what's fact and what is simply my perception of what's happening."

"Go on," said Bill, "I like what you're saying so far."

"If we're going to get our team to the national convention in six months, things have to change. Our numbers must come up, and we have to start working together as a cohesive team. I believe I've been guilty of jumping to my own conclusions and not communicating clearly with you guys. And as I just learned, I'm not always right. I had no idea that you were facing health challenges. I wish I'd known."

Jake stood up, walked toward Bill, and sat in the chair next to him. "Bill, I'm ready to hear what's going on in your life, not just in your career. I want us to be real teammates, not just two people working in the same office."

Bill hesitated for a moment, but then began, "I had a little heart problem – nothing more serious than a small blockage. It slowed me down for quite awhile until I finally had angioplasty during my vacation last month. Now the doc says I'm as good as new, but I admit, it did scare me and slow me down a bit."

"Are you going to be okay?" Jake said with concern.

"Yes, thank you. And bottom line, I love this job and want to show everyone that this old coot still has what it takes. Now that I feel better, I want the next few years to be my best ever. Then I can go out in a blaze of glory!"

Jake and Bill rose together and reached to shake each other's hands. "Let's do it then," said Jake, pulling Bill closer to him and hug/slapping him in the stiff but well-intentioned way guys often express positive emotion. Bill nodded and smiled in return as he left.

Jake leaned back in his chair reflecting on how far off he was with his assessment of Bill. He had thought Bill was lazy and ready for retirement when in reality he had taken his vacation time to have heart surgery.

Jake's Perspective Is A Tad Off

Jake decided to talk with Tad next, who was only a few months into his sales career but long overdue for a breakthrough in production. In fact, he'd yet to make a real sale completely on his own. Curious about the accuracy of his assumptions about Tad, he knocked on his office door.

Tad looked up at Jake with tense, timid eyes, expecting more of what he got from Jake at yesterday's meeting.

"Tad, I'd like your help," Jake asked.

"Sure," Tad responded, a little shaky. "What can I help you with?"

"My homework," said Jake with a hint of amusement.

"I beg your pardon?" Tad replied, somewhat startled.

"Never mind," said Jake as he searched for an appropriate way to express himself. "I get the feeling that something stops you from being as successful as you can be. I just wanted to check that with you."

Tad lowered his head and broke eye contact with Jake. Feeling busted, Tad decided this was the time to level with Jake – and himself.

"Jake, I know I can bring in big contacts because of my connections, but I have difficulty closing sales, and I am not, I just..." his voice trailed away.

"What do you think is missing?"

"Confidence I suppose," Tad replied. "Knowledge too. It's tough for me to admit this because I love this business. I just don't feel like I really know what I'm doing. I'm unsure of myself, and I don't have the sales expertise to close the deals. I need help if I'm going to make it in this business. I don't want to hold the team back, but I feel I'm doing exactly that."

Jake's eyes widened as Tad's façade melted before him. An insecure young man lived behind the polished veneer and nonchalant attitude! Who would have guessed it? Jake certainly hadn't seen beyond the public face Tad presented.

"Tad, you have excellent skills in every other area besides closing deals, right?" Tad nodded miserably. "I know we can help you acquire the knowledge and skills you need to become a top sales rep in this company. Let me give this some thought, and I'll come up with a plan to make it happen. Okay?"

"Sure," Tad smiled, feeling relieved. He had more to say, but Jake was already standing up and extending his hand.

Jake grinned and gave Tad's hand a firm shake. "It will take me a day or two because I'm pulling together a plan for the entire office team. In the meantime, you have appointments today, right?"

"Four of them."

"Great! Go get'em!"

The View From Left Field

Jake didn't have a chance to speak with Nathan that day, and conversations with Jean and Crystal didn't yield the satisfying breakthroughs he'd experienced with Bill and Tad.

Jean and her emotions remained a mystery to him. He'd read in some men's book that women are like oceans, ebbing and flowing with forces imperceptible to a land-locked man. Getting results out of Jean required more insight than that, but he couldn't do better at the moment. He did learn a few details about her son's run-ins with the law and could see how that would be destabilizing, but it still seemed like she spoke a different language. The competitive side of him was ashamed of his secret wish that she would leave – it would make things so much easier.

Crystal was a different story. The content of their conversation today was pretty good (they spoke mostly of her data base management system and personal goals), but Jake felt stiff-armed the whole time. He doubted she could ever lose her edge, but in the spirit of his homework he decided to keep an open mind. He'd played on a number of baseball teams that won even though all the players didn't like each other, so perhaps he could win with Crystal.

Thanks to a new set of lenses, Jake felt some optimism by the end of the day. The slump in his team's performance was not because they were lazy and unmotivated; that was only his perception and interpretation of the facts. *I guess I've really been out in left field on the real picture around here*, he thought to himself as he prepared to leave.

Jake remembered the old saying: You don't fully understand a person until you've walked a mile in his shoes. It was challenging for Jake to try on five different pairs of shoes (the women's were particularly uncomfortable – and not at all attractive on him), but he was determined to succeed. He felt he was off to a good start.

His mind then turned to Christine and wondered how all this applied to their relationship. He had thought they both understood each other well, but when he recalled their conversation from the night before, he wasn't so sure. "I thought you knew how I feel about you, Chris," he remembered saying. Then her reply hit him hard, "How would I know, Jake? Have you ever told me?"

The sense of pride he had previously felt from his good day at work evaporated, and a wave of sad realization rolled over him. *She's right, I've never told her.*

Comfortable Being Uncomfortable

Five days later Jake still had not re-connected with Christine. It was a lonely weekend, but at least now his apartment was clean. Throughout the week he made a conscious effort to notice the judgments he had about his staff and to investigate their accuracy. Although no "a-ha's" matched the two he had with Bill and Tad, a more grounded picture of each person's situation emerged.

One fact withstood any attack: The team's sales numbers were down. Jake could see that knowing his staff better (e.g., Jean is trying to quit smoking, and Crystal lost her father at an early age) could help him manage more effectively, but hey, we all have problems. They don't give us license to whine and complain. Focus and get the job done.

He also realized paying attention to his staff took time, and it certainly hadn't turned the team around yet.

That afternoon, Tuesday, Jake was fighting a fire again, this time helping Bill appease (and retain) one of their bigger accounts. It was a typical case of a client who declined a certain coverage and then blamed Freedom Mutual when his claim wasn't covered. After the flames died down, he dragged himself back to his office. As he plopped into his chair he glanced at the clock: 2:43 p.m.

"Argh!" Jake bellowed as he reached for the phone and dialed Coach's number. "I hope he's still around."

"I'm sorry to call you late, Coach," Jake apologized. "I had to help Bill save an account. I'm sure you understand."

"I appreciate your apology, Jake, and I do have some time now to talk before practice. Retirement has its advantages. We'll come back to your tardiness in a few minutes, but first I want to hear about your homework. What did you learn?"

Jake told the stories of his conversations with Bill, Tad, and his other team members. He concluded saying, "I can see the benefits of connecting with staff members. There seems to be a better flow of information. But on the other hand I can't say they are performing better, and it certainly isn't comfortable for me to be personal with them."

Coach smiled and nodded, "Lou Pinella, the Tampa Bay Devil Ray's manager, says he wants a team of guys that are 'comfortable being uncomfortable.' I like that line. I've found almost everything

I've found almost everything really valuable that I wanted in my life was sitting right outside of my comfort zone.

really valuable that I wanted in my life was sitting right outside of my comfort zone."

"I definitely have gotten outside of my comfort zone with my staff lately," said Jake.

"Way to go," said Coach. "I respect that. Now, in order to get your team members performing closer to their potential, you need to learn the fundamentals of work team communication," said Coach. "We're now ready to get into what I feel is the essence of doing business."

"Let's get started," Jake said eagerly. "I've got a long way to go and a short time to get there."

"You've already got a good start with the most fundamental element," Coach began, "realizing that you have a perspective, and that what you see and think isn't always the truth."

Jake nodded his head knowingly, "That first homework assignment was eye-opening, but I think it will be a long time until I can consistently remember that how things appear to me isn't necessarily how they are."

"Don't worry," smiled Coach. "You and the rest of us humans will work on that one for the rest of our lives. Just keep in mind that if you see your staff as lazy and incompetent, you almost assure that's how they'll be."

"I know: What I see is what I get."

"The next fundamental is **integrity**," Coach said. "Integrity can mean a lot of different things, but right now let's just define it as honoring your word: doing what you say you are going to do."

INTEGRITY
Honoring your word. Doing what you say you are going to do.

"Uh oh," said Jake, already sensing he was going to get hit hard by this fundamental.

Coach continued, "When you are *in* integrity, you have done what you said you would. When you operate in integrity, things work a lot better in your life. Good things happen. When you are *out* of integrity – when you say one thing but do another – things don't work so well."

"I've always felt I was a man of integrity, but now I'm not so sure," Jake said introspectively.

"That makes you normal," replied Coach. "Most people think they do what they say they are going to do, but until they really take a look at it (usually with someone else's help), they can't know for sure. In fact most people are out of integrity in a lot of places. You, for example, are out of integrity with me for calling late today."

"Uh, ya, I see that," stammered Jake.

"People in general don't pay close attention to how loosely they throw their word around. As a result they lose a lot of power without knowing it. Their lives just don't work very well, and they don't understand why. It's a stressful way to live. Have you got your notebook in front of you?"

"Yes," said Jake.

"Draw a full circle about the size of a golf ball to the left of center on a clean page. This circle is whole, it's complete, no breaks. It represents being in integrity. It's powerful; the energy it has inside stays inside. If you were rolling through life on a tire like this it would be a pretty smooth ride."

"Makes sense," Jake agreed.

"Just to the right of that circle draw another circle the same size, but don't complete it all the way, leave it open from about 2 o'clock to 4 o'clock. This represents being out of integrity. When you look at it, where does your eye immediately go?"

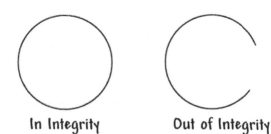

In Integrity   **Out of Integrity**

"To the gap," said Jake.

"Of course," Coach acknowledged, "and that's where all the energy goes, too. It leaks out the opening. This circle has no power. It can't be trusted. If you were taking a trip through your life on a tire like this it would be pretty unpleasant."

"That's me," said Jake, "I'm on a pretty bumpy ride right now."

"Yes, and you're blaming it on the road," Coach chuckled, "when the problem is actually your tire!"

Deep in thought, Jake scanned his life to see where he was out of integrity. He was unable to laugh along with Coach.

"Let's look at an example," Coach continued. "When you called me late for this phone call appointment, you paid a cost in three different areas. What do you think those three areas are?"

"I don't know," said Jake feeling the guilt clang in his belly, "but I'm sorry about all three."

"I'll help you out," said Coach. "You asked me to coach you. Were you getting any coaching between 2:00 p.m. and the time you called?"

"No."

"So the first and most obvious cost you pay when you are out of integrity is the **performance of the task** itself. This means you pay a price when whatever you had promised to do isn't done. If at work you broke a promise to complete a report by a certain time, the report wouldn't be done, and there would be consequences for that. If you promised to pick up Christine at seven and you didn't, she wouldn't get picked up at seven."

That line struck a nerve in Jake. "And that's not all that would happen!" he burst in.

"Oh," said Coach amused. "What else would be affected?"

"She wouldn't be too happy, and it would put a damper on the whole evening, to say the least. Things just don't seem to go as well when I don't show up on time."

"I'm not surprised," said Coach. "So the second cost of being out of integrity is the **trust in the relationship** between the people involved. When you're late, it affects how you and Christine relate to each other that evening, plus she will trust you less the next time you make a promise."

"That pretty much describes our whole relationship" Jake admitted. "She always gives me a funny look when I agree to a timetable with her, and I'm not sure I'll be able to recover from this last episode."

"Because she can't trust you," said Coach. "Trust is a performance fundamental. It can be defined as 'certainty based on past experience,' or simply a lack of fear. Whether you are talking about hitting, pitching, selling, dating, or anything else, the greater the trust, the closer you perform to your potential."

TRUST
A performance fundamental.
It can be defined as certainty based on past experience or simply a lack of fear.

"My relationship with Christine is certainly nowhere near its potential," bemoaned Jake.

"Sounds like she really gave it to you," said Coach.

"Big time," said Jake, her words still stinging his heart.

"Yes, but often people won't say anything to you when you break a promise, particularly in a business environment. They'll think it – even if it's only subconsciously – and it will register in their brains that you didn't do what you said you would. That memory puts some distance between you and them."

Not wanting to dwell on the distance it had put between him and Christine, Jake said, "So what's the third area?"

"How did you feel when you were apologizing to me for being late with this call?"

"Horrible," said Jake, rolling his eyes back. "I had a sinking feeling in my chest, a hollow feeling in my gut, and a little voice in my head calling me an idiot."

"Bingo," said Coach. "The third cost of being out of integrity is your **personal power,** or how you feel about yourself. Whether you are aware of it or not, your opinion of yourself takes a hit when you don't honor your word. One definition of self-esteem is the reputation you have with yourself. If you don't believe you'll do the things you promise, you don't feel good about yourself."

> *One definition of self-esteem is the reputation you have with yourself. If you don't believe you'll do the things you promise, you don't feel good about yourself.*

"I know that feeling," nodded Jake.

"When you are out of integrity, your body knows it and lets *you* know. You lose confidence. You lose happiness. You lose trust in yourself. Things go wrong in your personal and professional lives."

"I feel it in my gut," said Jake.

"We just spoke of the importance of trust between people wanting to perform well. The same applies on the personal level. When you don't trust yourself, you lose focus, tense up, and perform poorly. It doesn't get more fundamental than that."

"Ugh," Jake grunted, re-experiencing the hits he had taken lately, "I feel like I'd rather not even know this."

"I'll make it a bit worse before I make it better," said Coach. "I believe how a person does one thing is pretty much how that person does everything. So if you are out of integrity with Christine and with me, we can rest assured you are out of integrity at work."

> **How a person does one thing is pretty much how that person does everything.**

"I'm not so sure," hoped Jake.

Coach didn't feel the need to uncover specific examples of where Jake was out of integrity with his staff; he thought he'd let Jake see it for himself.

"Your word is your most important business asset, Jake. So when you tell me how poorly things are going at work, it's a pretty good bet that you and others are not operating in integrity."

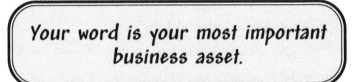

> **Your word is your most important business asset.**

Coach rolled on, picking up momentum, "And don't go thinking that you need to fix *them*, the problem starts with you. Too many leaders read some new book or bring in consultants to fix their people while thinking they themselves are so wonderful and enlightened. No team can outperform the limitations of its leader. Just like your perceptions limited your team, your integrity limits them. If you want your team to get better, *you* have to get better."

> No team can outperform the limitations of its leader. If you want your team to get better, you have to get better.

Silence followed as Coach let those last words resonate in Jake.

"Hey," said Coach, shifting the energy of the conversation, "You may have struck out a time or two lately, but that's the great thing about baseball and life, as long as you're still in the game you get to come up to bat again. Besides, many people never even become aware of the impact of their integrity. They don't understand why their lives don't work as well as they'd like. At least now you have a chance to do something about it."

"I feel a bit overwhelmed thinking about all this," said Jake.

"It takes courage to be in integrity, it definitely isn't the easy road."

"I guess," said Jake, "but I'm committed to moving ahead. What's my homework?"

"We've covered a lot," Coach answered. "I suggest you simply go to work tomorrow and notice where you are in or out of integrity. Look at things through a set of 'integrity lenses' so to speak. Like last time, don't try to be different or make any big changes, simply see what you notice when you become aware of your integrity and what it costs you to be out of integrity. You might also look at the effects of others' integrity."

Jake felt a bit better. After getting beaten up on his integrity, he recognized that doing his homework would again be beneficial.

"When should we talk again?" asked Jake.

"How about Friday?"

"Okay, let's try two o'clock again."

"Try?"

"Just kidding," said Jake. "I'll call you at 2:00 p.m. on Friday."

"Promise?"

"Yes," Jake smiled. "I haven't heard that one since I was a kid."

"Get used to it. It's a fundamental," said Coach. "We'll talk more about it soon, but I think you know what it means."

"Thanks, Coach."

It didn't take long after they hung up for Jake's thoughts to turn to Christine, but he decided to wait until after work to call her.

Making Contact

After work Jake went to his car, took out his cell-phone and dialed Christine's number. *Please answer, please answer*, he thought. On the third ring he heard a faint hello.

"Christine! Thanks so much for answering. I'm so sorry about last week, and I need to talk to you."

"Okay Jake, but I can't right now. I'm meeting Sophie for dinner in a few minutes, and I think we'll be out late. You can call me tomorrow night."

"Great," said Jake, "what time?"

"Anytime after 6:00 p.m. I should be home."

"I'll call you at 6:30 p.m.," said Jake, trying out his new integrity muscle. It went against his nature to pin himself down to a set time, but he knew he had to step up if he was going to win her back.

"We'll see about that," said Christine, with a skeptical tone.

After a moment of silence Jake whispered, "Christine, I love you." But she had already hung up the phone.

Are You In Or Out?

Jake got to the office early the next day. He remembered Coach told him not to try to do anything different, and that he should just be aware of his integrity, but that awareness drove him to make sure he wasn't late for work.

It felt good to arrive early. He used to always get to work early when he was selling full time. Somehow that had slipped since he started managing a sales team.

He searched for his yellow sticky pad under the piles of papers covering his desk. When he found it, he kept his homework reminder brief:

Integrity: In or Out

He was happy to have homework to distract him from thinking about his 6:30 p.m. call to Christine.

He cleaned up his desk. He had never promised anyone he would keep his desk clean, but somehow it felt out of integrity to have piles of paper strewn over his desktop. The piles certainly drained his energy.

Before launching into the to-do list for the day, Jake decided to review his notes from yesterday's conversation with Coach. Integrity affects:

- My **performance** on the task.
- **Trust** others will have in me.
- My **personal power**.

He then decided to inventory his commitments in his notebook. *Where am I out of integrity, and what's it costing me?* The answers came slowly at first, then picked up speed.

Certainly the low-hanging fruit on this list is my chronic tardiness, Jake thought. *Coach was right. That doesn't just happen with Christine; I'm usually late for meetings here, too, especially with staff. But it's part of the whole culture at Freedom Mutual. People understand that. Everyone is late, aren't they? Besides, what difference does it make?* Let's look at the costs:

> **Performance:** I lose meeting time. The team doesn't cover anything on the agenda when I'm not there. But I usually get some task done while I'm not there, so that balances that out. On the

other hand, the staff is sitting there waiting, so they get nothing done.

Trust: I've never really thought it through. I'm the manager and we start when I get there. That's the way my managers were, and that's how it is when my boss has his staff meetings. People just accept it. But that's *my* perspective! I need to check this one out. I'll ask Bill. He's a real on-time guy, I'll find out what effect it has on him.

Personal Power: I'm usually pretty stressed going into the meetings. That's not fun. I haven't felt too bad about it before, but now I do.

Being late is one place I'm out of integrity, Jake exhaled. *Let's see if I can find another.*

The Henderson prospect came to mind. Jake had been given a referral by one of his best customers and promised to call the prospect last Friday, but hadn't. He got caught up in the day's events and thought it would be okay if he made the call Monday. Now it was Wednesday. *I broke a promise,* Jake thought to himself. The cost? Let's see:

Performance: Obviously I don't have the bid out, so I can't get the business. That's potentially costing money for my team and me.

Trust: There might not be much credibility lost with the prospect if he doesn't know I'm to call him. But if Henderson told the prospect I'd call

Friday, I will have lost this guy's trust. J. Robert Henderson will certainly give his referrals to someone else if he doesn't think I'm going to act on them.

Personal Power: I feel embarrassed and anxious. That's not good. I see what Coach means by losing personal power when I'm out of integrity. I wouldn't want to go into an important meeting feeling like this.

Jake resisted his urge to call the prospect right then: it was too early. But he promised this guy would get a call by 10:00 a.m. today.

"That's two places I'm out of integrity," said Jake out loud, hoping that's all he would come up with. It wasn't.

He had promised to complete his staff's written work evaluations by now, but hadn't even started them. He had told Tad he would give him additional training on closing deals, but hadn't. He had promised to have a sales meeting detailing the company's newest products. He hadn't. *Ugh,* Jake thought, *this is terrible.*

Jake shifted to the personal side. *I promised myself I would work out three times a week this year, but I'm not even getting in two.* Jake realized that in addition to the lost energy and self-esteem, there was a financial cost to this one. He'd have to buy new pants pretty soon because the ones he had were getting pretty tight.

That's more than enough about me, thought Jake. *Let's look at the integrity of my staff members.*

Bill was a man of his word, and his clients really appeared to trust him completely. In addition to his experience, Bill's integrity was why Jake felt safe asking for his advice on difficult matters. *Integrity equals trust. Trust determines performance.*

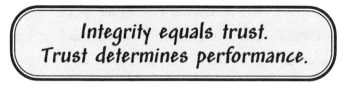

**Integrity equals trust.
Trust determines performance.**

Bill closed a majority of his sales calls, and now that his ticker was on the mend, his numbers will go up. Although Jake wondered about Bill's integrity in not telling him sooner about his heart condition, Jake respected his choice.

Jean came across to her clients as compassionate, but too often lost accounts by being unreliable and unprofessional. She was not making the number of cold calls she said she would and was almost always late with the weekly report, each time justifying it with some wild story about what was going on at home. She was a crisis waiting to happen. Do some people just have bad karma, or does she somehow create these situations?

Tad, on the other hand, always appeared to work off other people and take credit for their sales. No integrity in that. Jake felt better about Tad since their talk, but wished Tad had come forward sooner. Jake was in no position to criticize, though, he had originally promised Tad more training weeks ago and hadn't delivered.

Then there was Crystal. She was currently the top producer on the staff, and he couldn't find fault in her integrity with her clients. The problem was her inability to get along with the other sales reps in the office. She was catty, abrasive, and made fun of them behind their backs. That seemed out of integrity to Jake, but she's never promised she wouldn't be that way. Jake made a note to ask Coach about this type of integrity.

Finally there was Nathan. Something of a freeloader riding on Daddy's coat tails, Nathan never seemed to commit to anything, so how could he be out of integrity?

Jake had essentially known how he felt about each of his staff members before this exercise, but using integrity as the lens through which he viewed them made things clearer. He noticed that he respected each of his staff to the degree they operated in integrity. He thought of calling a staff meeting to share what he had learned, but remembered Coach's advice to work on the tool user first. *The way I've*

> **He noticed that he respected each of his staff to the degree they operated in integrity.**

acted lately they would probably laugh if I preached to them about integrity, he thought to himself. *Besides, I'd probably be late to the meeting.*

Remembering the conversation he wanted to have with Bill, Jake put his pen down and headed for Bill's office.

"Have you got a moment, Bill?" Jake asked after knocking on Bill's office door. "I want to check something with you."

"Sure," said Bill, enjoying Jake's new interest in his opinions.

"I know I'm almost always late to our staff meetings, and I'd like to know what effect that has on the staff."

"Well, ah, we know you're busy and things come up," Bill offered as a trial balloon. "We know you get there when you can."

"Come on, Bill," said Jake, his B.S. detector going off. "I really want to know."

"Okay," said Bill. "It costs you a lot, actually – credibility, respect. Sometimes people make snide remarks about you while we sit there. It seems like a power play. You make us wait because you can. We know we come second to whatever you're doing. Other than that it doesn't matter."

Bill sarcastically added that last line in a weak attempt to lighten his message. He could tell by the look on Jake's face that he could use some lightening.

"I see," said Jake. "That's not good. But thank you, I appreciate your being straight with me."

Jake's to-do list grew throughout the day as he recognized more and more promises he had made and not fulfilled. At the end of the day, he had seen enough of the cost of being out of integrity. He knew he wanted to be in integrity and get his staff to do the same. He just didn't know how.

But that's where Coach came in. Jake was happy to have Coach in his corner. It felt good to have a powerful ally outside of the organization so he didn't have to worry about political repercussions for anything he talked about. Besides, Michael Jordan had a coach, and Tiger Woods has a coach, as do many top athletes and executives. All great performers do.

Making The Call

Jake considered calling Coach before he called Christine. It was now 6:16 p.m., and after a day of looking in an integrity mirror he wasn't feeling very powerful. Instead he imagined how he wanted the conversation to go, and vigilantly watched the clock creep toward 6:30 p.m.

He drew a deep breath as the big moment arrived, and was thrilled to hear her voice. He began rattling off his thoughts at break-neck speed.

"Christine, I'm sorry I was late the other night, and I know you are upset about how absorbed I've been with work, and you question whether I care about my staff, but let me assure you...."

"Jake!" Christine interrupted, "I don't believe that you even understand what I'm upset about. The issue is I can't trust you. I'm not upset about what you do at work. I'm upset about what you do, and don't do, with *me*. For the past two years, time after time you haven't followed through on what you said you would do. In fact, you often don't commit to anything at all, including our relationship. I'm not sure why I've put up with it as long as I have."

"I know exactly what you're talking about," exclaimed Jake, "that's exactly what I've been working on! You're right. You've complained about it many times, but I didn't understand what you meant. Now I do, and I want a chance to prove it to you."

"You've said that before and nothing changed, Jake. How many times do you think I'll fall for it?"

"I called on time tonight, didn't I? I see this as a whole new ballgame and I'm now one for one!"

A cascade of feelings came over Christine: anger at having been left waiting so many times, frustration over not knowing whether or not to give him another chance, and love for the son-of-a-gun.

"I need more time, Jake," Christine said abruptly. "You can call me again in a week."

"If that's what you want. I will definitely call you in a week," said Jake, feeling a strange mix of disappointment and hope.

Shortly after hanging up the phone it occurred to him that it was probably good that he would get another week to learn more about integrity and get his act together. *That's the perspective I'll choose*, he thought to himself.

PART THREE

❖

The Integrity
Tools

Further Opening Jake

"Good stuff, Jake," said Coach. "Those are some powerful insights. I can tell when someone plays full-out on their homework because they make observations that go beyond what we have previously discussed."

Jake had requested a marathon session with Coach to help speed his learning. He was now racing two deadlines: getting his team performing well enough to qualify for the convention in New York, and more importantly, getting his integrity to where Christine would take him back before she completely washed him out of her heart. He and Coach met after Little League practice in a place they were both most comfortable—the dugout.

"As I see it," said Coach, "there are two levels of integrity. The first is being true to your word. The second is being true to yourself; in other words, behaving in a way that is consistent with your values. You did a nice job of picking up on that second level. For example, order is a value of yours. Having a messy desk costs you energy. You created order

> **There are two levels of integrity. The first is being true to your word; the second is being true to yourself.**

when you cleaned it up. Crystal is being catty and making fun of others behind their backs, and that also violates your values of honesty and respect."

"I've always known it wasn't good to bust on people when they weren't around," said Jake, "but I'd never really considered just how destructive it is."

"Just like not keeping your word drains your energy," Coach continued, "living outside your values drains your energy. Integrity is a value, but it's also a universal performance principle. I've yet to find someone whose life works better when they are out of integrity than when they are in integrity."

> **Integrity is a value, but it's also a universal performance principle.**

Despite the poor numbers his sales team had produced to date and the sorry state of his relationship with Christine, Jake felt a sense of pride. He was learning, gaining traction, and again had a sense of possibility. But one thing still bothered him.

"I would have liked Bill and Tad to tell me with their issues long before I asked them," Jake said. "I have an open-door policy, so I don't fully understand why they didn't let me help them sooner."

"The door isn't the issue," said Coach. "It's how accessible and open they perceive you to be; how much they trust you and feel you care about them. You don't need an open door policy, you need an open Jake policy."

"I see," nodded Jake.

Coach continued, "A lot of managers hide behind an open door policy thinking it covers the human relationship side of performance. But actually the more your staff believes that you care about them, the better they will respond when you challenge them, and the more information you will get from them – information that is critical to your making good decisions."

Jake thought of Christine's questioning of how much he cared about his staff. "We could have gotten much better numbers out of Tad if I had known what was going on with him sooner," he said.

"A lot of sports coaches make tough demands on their players," said Coach, "but the ones who create sustained excellence challenge their players while at the same time establishing in their minds that they actually care about them as individuals. In business the

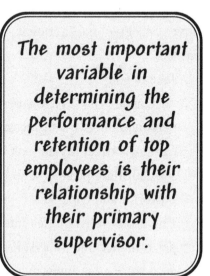

The most important variable in determining the performance and retention of top employees is their relationship with their primary supervisor.

research is pretty clear that the most important variable in determining the performance and retention of top employees is their relationship with their primary supervisor."

"So the more they perceive that I care, the more I can challenge them," said Jake.

"Yes."

"Well, I'd better pick up the care level because we have a big challenge ahead," said Jake.

"That's not something I can tell you how to do, Jake. You either care or you don't."

"Got it," said Jake. "So let's get to these tools you mentioned earlier."

"So far we've focused on building your awareness of some performance fundamentals," Coach said. "Before we move on, give me a quick summary of what you've learned."

Jake began:

- "I'm aware that I have a perspective, and that how I perceive things isn't necessarily the truth, but it will certainly affect my actions. My perspective becomes a self-fulfilling prophecy, so I better see my staff as powerful and capable.

- I'm also now aware that integrity plays a crucial role in performance and in personal happiness too. If performance were a car, integrity would be the tires. When I am in integrity the ride can be pretty smooth. When I am out of integrity it will be a rough ride, and I may not even get to where I want to go.

* And now I understand how important actually caring is. I want to connect with people on a personal level."

"Great," said Coach, "and caring doesn't mean you have to dig into their private lives or be buddy-buddy with them. They just need to believe you care."

"Showing up on time is a way of showing I care."

"Indeed," said Coach, "and the tools I'm about to share with you can be seen as manipulative unless you use them with care, respect and dignity."

"I promise I will," said Jake.

Loud And Clear

Just then a young boy meekly emerged from behind the dugout. It was Peter Illig, one of the boys on Coach's team. His head was down and his eyes were red and puffy from recent tears.

"Coach, can you help me?" asked Peter.

"Peter," said Coach, "of course. What are you still doing here?"

"My parents haven't come to pick me up."

"Oh," said Coach sympathetically, "that's no fun."

"It's like the fourth time it's happened," said Peter.

"Who was supposed to pick you up?" asked Coach.

"I don't know," said Peter.

"I'm sure we can take care of it," said Coach. He pulled out his phone list and called the boy's father, who said he was nearby and would come immediately.

Coach took the opportunity to help Peter learn from the situation. "I suggest you talk to your parents about how we teach you to communicate on fly balls in the outfield. Remember, we always want one player to call out, 'I got it' loud and clear so everyone else gets out of the way and there are no mix-ups."

"Yes," said Peter, his spirits lifting, "I caught three fly balls today."

"And I heard you call all three of them loudly and clearly," added Coach.

Coach then encouraged Peter to be a **player** and communicate clearly with his parents. "I know at 10-years-old you can't drive yourself, so you really don't control whether you get picked up or not. But you can take responsibility for making sure one of them promises to pick you up."

"Okay," said Peter, "I'll make sure one of them says, 'I got him' before I leave for practice."

"Loud and clear," said Coach.

"Loud and clear," repeated Peter.

A few minutes later Peter's dad pulled up. He yelled through his open window, "Sorry, I thought his mom was going to pick him up."

Coach and Jake just waved and smiled politely. In a hushed voice Coach asked Peter, "When will you talk to your parents about what we just talked about?"

"I'll do it right now," said Peter as he ran toward his dad's car and hopped in.

"Wow," said Jake. "There it is. Peter's parents were out of integrity."

"Yes," said Coach, "and not because they are bad people. They just don't communicate clearly. They, like most groups, lack rigor in the fundamentals."

"Seems to me you were just starting to tell me how I could do better with that at the office," said Jake.

"Yes," said Coach, his eyes lighting up with enthusiasm. "Let's get a drink of water and stretch a bit so we're sharp for this next topic."

Into The Gap

"The Integrity Tools I'm going to teach you will make it easier for you to create a high performance culture of integrity and accountability," said Coach as they walked back to their seats in the dugout. "They make up a system you can use to simultaneously care about your staff and challenge them. Let's put that performance car of yours into gear!"

Jake opened his notebook and got his pen ready.

"I recall you said you recently upgraded the operating system on your computers at the office," said Coach. "What did that do for you?"

"We're still adjusting," said Jake, "but regardless of what program we're running it enhances the speed, power, and reliability of all our systems."

"Okay, well you and your staff have what I refer to as an *interpersonal operating system*. Regardless of what they are working on, their operating system is their norm for the way they interact, coordinate actions, and communicate. Implementing these tools is like upgrading the group's interpersonal operating system. It enhances the integrity of your team processes."

"So we'll work faster, more effectively, and with fewer crashes," replied Jake.

"Exactly," Coach continued. "The key to this upgrade and being in integrity is clarity. Clarity increases power.

Clarity increases power.

Everything we'll talk about from here on is designed to help you be clear in your communication. Remember, you each see the conversation through your own set of lenses, your own perspective. You each have different motivations, histories, beliefs, and feelings. You each are dealing with different emotions. The tools I'll give you will help you cut through all that and reduce the possibility that you will misunderstand each other. They also maximize the chances for excellent performance."

Jake nodded. He knew he needed help filtering through all the noise created by the interpersonal differences on his team.

"The first step is to define the **gap**," said Coach. "The key questions are: Where do things stand now? And what would you like to have happen?"

"Right now we are in the 25th percentile in sales at Freedom Mutual," said Jake. "We have a reasonably

**GAP
The difference between where things stand now and where you would like them to be.**

talented group that lacks focus and integrity, and we have a motivated leader."

"And what would you like to have happen?" asked Coach.

"I want the whole team to go to the convention in New York City in November. That only happens if we are in the top ten percent of the company by the first day of October. I'd like that to be accomplished by a team working well together, trusting each other, and feeling good about themselves."

"It usually takes longer for someone to get that much clarity on their gap," said Coach, impressed.

"I've been thinking about this instead of sleeping lately," said Jake.

"So does your team know this is your goal?" asked Coach.

"They should, but I also thought Christine knew how I feel about her. So I'd say no, they probably don't."

DECLARATION
A statement of your commitment.

"So step two is to make a **declaration** about what you are committed to making happen."

"Like the Declaration of Independence?" said Jake.

"Yes," responded Coach. "The colonists declared themselves free from England. Then they had to win the war for independence. John F. Kennedy declared America would go to the moon in the 1960s, and then the scientists had to make it happen. That's the game: Make a declaration and then chase after it – make it true in reality and not just in your word. With no declaration, there's no game. If you aren't getting the results you want, you either haven't made a declaration, or you're not living consistently with a declaration you have made. Either way you are out of integrity."

"Setting a goal, essentially," said Jake.

"Yes, and declare it as true, then live consistently with its truth as opposed to saying it is something you *hope* will happen. Then it becomes a matter of integrity.

"Will you act consistently with your declaration?" Coach continued, "I've found that the better job you do of keeping your word on small things on a daily basis, the better job you'll do on making your big declarations a reality. It's as if you build an integrity muscle,

> *The better job you do of keeping your word on small things on a daily basis, the better job you'll do on making your big declarations a reality.*

and you get more powerful at making your word become

reality. Also, the universe supports people better when they live in integrity."

"The universe?" asked Jake.

"We can talk about that later," said Coach, respecting Jake's desire to move quickly. "So let's hear it. What is your declaration regarding your team?"

"We are going to the convention in New York as a team this fall because we are in the top ten percent of sales reps for Freedom Mutual!"

"How does that feel?" asked Coach.

"Good. Scary, and a stretch, but good."

"So by when will you share this with your team?" asked Coach.

"We have a staff meeting tomorrow, I'll do it then."

Gap

↓

Declaration

"Great," said Coach pulling out a sheet of paper and sketching out the first two steps of a diagram.

"So now you have a gap and have made a declaration," said Coach. "What do you need in order to fulfill on that declaration?"

"Help!" joked Jake.

"Exactly," replied Coach, catching Jake off guard.

"When You're Feeling Stressed..."

Coach continued, "And what is a caring, respectful way to get someone to help you?"

"Ask, I suppose."

"Great, so the next step is called making a **request**," said Coach, drawing the third step of his diagram.

> **REQUEST**
> The act of asking for a promise.

Gap
↓
Declaration
↓
Request

"As you saw with Bill and Tad," Coach continued, "people aren't always willing to make requests, even if it seems obvious that help from others would improve their situation significantly. What do you think stops people, particularly in business settings, from making requests?"

"Fear, I'd say," said Jake. "Fear of looking stupid or weak. I know I don't enjoy asking for help. Actually, despite my struggles lately I didn't go to my boss for help. And when I put myself in Tad's shoes, I could understand not asking for sales training help. He seemed pretty humbled as he told me about it."

"Yes," said Coach, "most organizations hold looking good and knowing things as top values, and so people think twice about opening themselves up to ask for assistance. This is pretty ironic since the best way to look good is to produce great results, and the best way to do that is with help from others."

"I'm certainly a lot better off now that I've asked you to help me," said Jake. "So somehow I need to get to where I can swallow my pride and make requests and become a manager whose staff feels comfortable making requests to."

"If you want different results, you need to be different," said Coach. "Here's a slogan for you:

When you're feeling stressed,
make a request.

"When you are under the gun or you have a big gap like the one you defined earlier," Coach continued, "instead of only using personal resources, think of a request you could make that would help ease your pain."

"And then actually make the request," Jake added.

"Yes," said Coach. "The first mistake people in companies tend to make is that they don't ask for help when they need it. Their egos and need to be right stop them from reaching out to others.

"The second mistake they make is they don't actually make a clear request. They make declarations about what they want and let the people they talk with infer what the request is. For example, they might say, *We need to get the TechCom portfolio done,* but stop short of clarifying who is to do what and by when."

"I've certainly done that," admitted Jake. "So what makes a clear request?"

"A good place to start," said Coach, "is to give the person the context for **why** you are making the request. What is the situation you are in—what is your gap? That way they can see the importance of the request. It gives the task meaning. Also, giving them the bigger picture creates the possibility that they will have a better idea for how to produce the ultimate result you want. It's a more respectful and more effective way to start instead of simply telling them what you want."

"Makes sense," said Jake.

"Now," Coach continued, "keep in mind the goal is to operate in integrity. It's pretty hard to close the loop on a task when you aren't clear on who is supposed to do what and by when. Lack of clarity is one of the biggest causes of poor integrity and poor performance in organizations."

"And of young children being left waiting after baseball practices," mused Jake.

"Yes," said Coach. "So the bottom line is you need to get clear on who you want to do what by when. The basic formula is: *I request that you do X by Y*."

Jake was busy writing these words in his notebook. "Who will do what by when? I've certainly heard that one before."

> *Get clear on who you want to do what by when.*

Coach continued, "How many times have you either been in someone else's meeting or your own, and after hours of talking walked out pretty confident nothing would significantly change before the next time you met?"

"Let's see," said Jake with tongue in cheek, "how many meetings have I had this week?"

Coach grinned, "So a powerful request includes who you want to do what and by when. As I said, adding *why* up front is also a good idea so people understand the context for the task. They might come up with a different way to accomplish it."

"It sounds like being that thorough will take a lot more time," Jake responded.

"Not when you compare it to the time it takes to be inefficient or let time go by without any work being done. How about the amount of time it takes to do something two or even three times?"

"I hear you," agreed Jake.

Promises, Promises

"Now for the last piece for the day," said Coach. "When you make a request, there are only four responses you should accept. What do you think they are?"

"*Yes* and *no* seem like safe bets," said Jake. "They're pretty clear."

"You're two for two," said Coach.

"Although I will say that in our company culture, people don't feel no is an option," Jake said.

"If you can't say no, then it isn't a request; it's a command," Coach explained. "Commands – telling someone what to do – lack dignity and respect, so while it might produce short-term results, it won't create sustainable excellence. I want to get the basics covered today, so let's put that topic on hold and see if you can come up with the other two acceptable responses to a request right now."

"How about asking clarifying questions?" Jake asked. "I'm often not clear what my boss wants when he gives me instructions."

"It's always a good idea to ask for clarification. Remember: Clarity is power. The more clarity you have on the issue the better. But once you are both clear, you still need to get one of the four responses, so asking a clarifying question doesn't count as one of the four."

"The typical answers I hear around the office are: 'We'll see,' 'Maybe,' 'I'm not sure' and 'I'll see what I can do.' Sometimes I hear nothing. Sometimes I send email requests to my boss that just seem to disappear into some vortex. None of those is very clear, so I'm not going to guess any of them."

"Excellent choice, Grasshopper," Coach smirked.

"I think you gave me one earlier when you suggested I could propose a different idea," said Jake. "Sort of saying, 'I know you'd like me to do X by Y, but how about if I do Z by Y instead?'"

"Very good, I call that a **counter offer**, that's three. One more…"

> COUNTER OFFER
> A proposed alternative
> to a request.

Jake thought for a few moments. "May I phone a friend?" he quipped.

"If I let you do that, by when would you get back to me?" said Coach.

"Ah, ha," said Jake, catching Coach's clue. "So if I don't want to commit to an answer at the moment of the request, I can commit to responding at some set time in the future."

"Exactly. You may need to check your calendar or the availability of your resources before you can properly respond to a request. But instead of the usual, *I'll get back to you,* agree to a particular time by when you will respond."

On his notepad, Jake wrote out the four responses that are acceptable to a request:

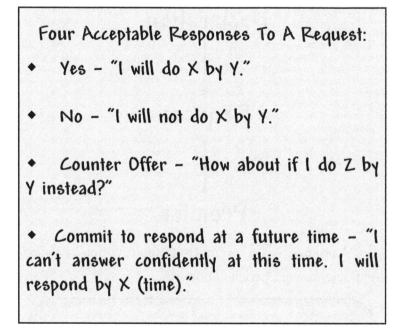

Four Acceptable Responses To A Request:

♦ Yes – "I will do X by Y."

♦ No – "I will not do X by Y."

♦ Counter Offer – "How about if I do Z by Y instead?"

♦ Commit to respond at a future time – "I can't answer confidently at this time. I will respond by X (time)."

Coach nodded his agreement, "If you accept anything else, you're asking for trouble."

Jake continued to write as Coach went on, "Ultimately the goal of a request is to get a **promise**. A promise is also a matter of who will do what by when. The basic formula is: 'I will do X by Y.'"

Coach drew the next piece of the Integrity Tools Model:

Gap
Declaration
Request
Promise

"A promise is a commitment to future action in a specified time frame," Coach continued.

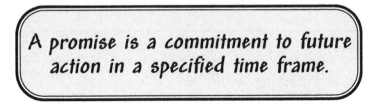

A promise is a commitment to future action in a specified time frame.

"Personal power and success are determined by your ability to make and fulfill promises. Your personal reputation and the reputation of your organization depend on your ability to make and fulfill promises. Fulfillment of promises breeds trust. Non-fulfillment of promises breeds distrust."

> **Personal power and success are determined by your ability to make and fulfill promises.**

"I'm often afraid to make a commitment because I'm afraid I won't be able to fulfill it," Jake replied.

"Granted, making a promise puts your integrity at risk, but not making promises makes you powerless. You have to choose what works best for you. Let me ask you though, would you want to work for someone afraid to make promises?"

Jake didn't feel the need to respond.

"And keep in mind," Coach continued, "there's a big difference between making a mistake and telling a lie. It is a mistake when you break a promise you thought you could and would fulfill. No one fulfills all his or her promises. Life gets in the way sometimes. But it's a lie if you make a promise knowing full well you can't or won't fulfill it. With a mistake, something unforeseen happens. With a lie you knew from the start you would not fulfill the request."

"I see," Jake nodded.

"The dance between requests and promises is at the heart of performance, trust, and personal power," said Coach. "It may sound simple, but it is anything but easy.

All the complexities of individual human emotions, egos, perspectives, politics, fears and personal histories make clear communication and operating in integrity very difficult in organizations. But understanding the fundamentals makes it as easy as possible, and that's what we've introduced today."

Jake knew Coach was right. Requests and promises seemed straightforward. It seemed obvious that this would result in work getting done, but it certainly wasn't the way things ran at his office.

"So what are you walking away with from our conversation today?" asked Coach.

"First is the importance of caring and respecting my staff, and connecting with them."

"Good," said Coach. "The mechanics of requests and promises are of little value if caring and respect don't form the context for the relationship."

"And then what stands out is the idea of who will do what by when."

> Manager: "I request that you do X by Y"
> Team Member: "Yes, I will do X by Y."

"Okay," said Coach, "and keep in mind everything we're talking about requires practice to implement, so don't worry about getting it all right now. It's the same as when I showed you how to throw a curveball back when you played ball. You did okay from the start but got very good through practice and coaching."

Jake recalled having some of his early curveballs hit out of the park, but by the end of his career it was his best pitch.

"As for your homework," said Coach, "in addition to making your declaration to your team, apply your understanding of requests and promises as best you can. When we get together the next time, we'll talk through the inevitable breakdowns that occur. For now, just focus on getting clear on who will do what by when."

Jake's head was full, and he felt challenged to take in all this new information. But as he always had, Coach simplified things quite a bit. Define a gap, make a declaration, make requests and get promises. Get clarity on who will do what by when.

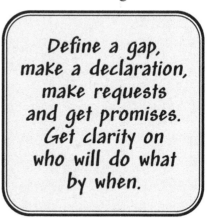

Define a gap, make a declaration, make requests and get promises. Get clarity on who will do what by when.

As Jake drove off, he smiled and felt optimistic about tomorrow's staff meeting. He wished he could call Christine to share what he had learned.

Stepping Up To The Plate

The next morning at 8:45 a.m., Jake sat in the conference room prepared and waiting for his sales team. He repeated over and over in his head, *Who will do what by when? Who will do what by when? Exaggerate it today. Be loud and clear.*

One by one they entered, each looking at Jake and then the clock, especially Crystal, who seemed shocked by Jake's promptness.

As soon as everyone was seated, Jake began the meeting. "We are going to the national convention this fall," he said proudly, "as a team." The group looked at Jake and then each other with befuddlement. A few muted chortles popped out, none of the staff certain if they were laughing with or at Jake.

"Do they need us to work the check-in booth?" cracked Tad, getting a few laughs.

"I know it may sound like a stretch, and that's because it *is* a stretch. But I'm seeing things with a different perspective now, and I believe we have the necessary talent in this room to pull it off. I want you all to see what I see. You are all capable of being in the top ten percent of Freedom Mutual. Bill has been there before, and so have I. It's not just about the trip, it's about the feeling of satisfaction that comes with knowing you are one of the best, and that you closed the gap between where you were and where you wanted to be."

"The bonus check is a plus too," added Bill.

"It's a fantastic feeling," Jake continued, "and I want you all to experience it. This is the year all of us will experience it together."

Crystal rolled her eyes and muttered, "Yeah, right," but Jake chose not to comment and continued.

"I know we have the players we need to make it. The key is to work together in order to achieve this goal. Obviously we have to start doing some things differently. We're all going to have to step up to the plate and execute the fundamentals."

As he spoke, Jake was getting excited, but nervous. He could visualize the team reaching this goal, but he still had plenty of doubt. Jake had been thinking about Coach's emphasis on respecting his staff, so instead of telling them his strategy, Jake decided to request they come up with their own ideas first. *Now that I'm feeling stressed,* he thought to himself, *it's time to make a request.*

"I've got some ideas on how we can do this," he said out loud, "but there's a lot of great experience and brainpower in this room, so I want your ideas first. We're going to meet back here tomorrow at this same time. In the meantime, I request that you do some homework. Start with a little self-analysis: What are you good at? And what are you not so good at? Where are you strong? Where are you weak? What would you need help with if you were going to raise your productivity by 50 percent? Be ready to request help in your weakest areas. I'd also like you to come up with ideas for how we can double our commission dollars over the next six months. So my request is that you each show up here tomorrow morning at nine o'clock ready to brainstorm and make firm commitments for what you will do and by when."

Everyone sat in silence, still in mild shock.

"One thing I can tell you that has to be different," said Jake, "is the way we communicate. We need to do a much better job with our communication fundamentals and be much cleaner and clearer in our speaking and in our commitments. So you can ask me clarifying questions if you have any. Then I'll be listening to each of you for one of four answers to my homework request. You can say yes, no, propose a counter offer, or commit to respond at a set time in the future."

They could see Jake was serious. Something had obviously shifted in him. He looked like the same guy that had chewed them out just a few days ago, but he didn't sound like the same fellow. Silently they questioned: What is with this word *request?* Was it the magic word for the day? It certainly was a new one in his vocabulary.

One by one each person agreed to Jake's request, promising to do his or her homework and be back at 9:00 a.m. tomorrow.

"Great," said Jake. "Thank you. The last thing I want to say today is that I want this team to operate in integrity. All that we need to do is say what we are going to do and then do it. I know I've been as bad as anyone about this, so I certainly can't throw any stones on this issue. But now that I understand the cost of being out of integrity, of not doing what I promised, I'm committed to changing the relationship between what I say and what I do.

> **Now that I understand the cost of being out of integrity, of not doing what I promised, I'm committed to changing the relationship between what I say and what I do.**

I request your help with this. If there is anything I promised you that I haven't delivered, please let me know."

With that comment the meeting ended, and each person left the room curious about what tomorrow would bring.

Getting Their Feet Wet

One thing the next day brought was rain. Traffic was bad enough in the Capital District on a normal day, but by adding a steady rain commuting time could easily double. Things backed up on the Beltway, and Jean (the Drama Queen) was fifteen minutes late for the meeting.

Jake started the meeting by teaching the staff the fundamentals of requests and promises and asked them all to use these Integrity Tools in their discussion today. "It might seem pretty basic to speak this way," he concluded as Jean slogged in, soaked, "but if we were good at it, we wouldn't be in the bottom half of sales for the company."

Then Jake re-stated his declaration for the team. He also reiterated the fact that they would need to double their commission income over the next six months in order to qualify for the national sales convention. It was a huge undertaking, but Jake was excited and committed to achieving it. Making it to the convention and raising their production was no longer simply about him and saving his job. It was now – finally – about the team.

"Yesterday you accepted my request to come up with some ideas to help us fulfill my declaration. What did you come up with? What do you think we could do differently in order to achieve our goal?"

Silence. As if choreographed, they all looked down at the table in front of them. No one wanted to speak first. Either no one trusted *New Jake* or no one wanted to be the brown-noser that spoke first.

They were all surprised, and Jake was relieved, when Nathan, the skinny young man, broke the tension with a nervous voice. "You all probably think I'm the weakest link here and not a very good salesperson. If that's what you think, you're right. You also know that if I weren't the CEO's nephew, I probably would have been booted out of here a long time ago. I know that too. But even though I'm not good at this job, I do really like all of you and care about what happens to this team."

Where is this going? they all thought, but out of courtesy didn't say.

"Anyway," he continued, his voice gradually lowering as he became more comfortable, "I don't care much for sales. The truth is, what I really like is number crunching, details, and statistics."

They all noticed how his eyes lit up as he began to talk about numbers and details. They shook their heads because statistics bored them to tears.

"I've been reviewing the numbers," Nathan continued, "and I've also analyzed all of our previous business for the past five years and made graphs and detailed plans of renewals, births, and changes needed for these plans. If I calculated correctly, we can generate half of our goal just by contacting these existing clients and updating their contracts."

Jake was flabbergasted, as was everyone else in the room. Nathan must have been up all night working on these graphs and plans, and it was genius to boot!

Nathan continued, "If it's okay with you, I'd like to continue to work on my analysis for 10 and 15 years back because I think there's a gold mine of opportunity for sales there."

"Nathan," said Jake, still taken aback, "great job investigating these accounts. What does everyone else think?"

After noting total agreement from the team, Jake continued. "So what's the best way to proceed?"

"It's not rocket science," said Bill after a brief pause. "We divvy up the assignments, call the clients to set up appointments, and get going."

Jake was getting ready to pounce with his first 'Who will do what by when?' but instead said, "You guys, I just had one of those deja-vu experiences. I feel like we've been here before. I mean the point where we all get excited about something and seem to agree on taking an action, but then we don't follow through. Does anyone else remember this happening?"

"I can't speak for anyone else," said Jean, "but I know it happens to me. I may have the best intentions to make cold calls, but then something happens in my life or the phone rings and before I know it, the day goes by and I didn't make any new appointments."

"And that's the only way we can get our numbers up," said Bill. "We have to put new prospects in the pipeline or up-sell to existing customers. I sure could use some help making calls. I just don't have enough time to make them."

"Yes," said Jake, "I bet every one of us has something that gets in the way of picking up the phone and making those calls." To his surprise, Jake saw Tad shaking his head in disagreement out of the corner of his eye. *Of all people,* Jake thought to himself, *Tad should be the last one to disagree because he hasn't closed one sale on his own. He's still stuck in his act pretending he's got it all together. But I'd better check and see if my perception is fact or fiction.*

"Tad," Jake said aloud, "looks like you don't agree with what we are saying. Is that true?"

"Actually, no," said Tad. "It's just different for me. I don't mind making calls. As you know I have a lot of strong leads and contacts. I enjoy making the calls, and I'm good at it. However, I don't feel like I've had any training or mentoring on how to close a sale."

His voice gained a bit of an edge and he continued. "When I first agreed to work for you, Jake, you agreed to teach me the business. That never happened. So here we are, and I feel like the weakest link on the team."

Jake kept his I've-got-it-together face on, but inside he was scrambling. It was certainly easier to tell people what to do than it was to let them speak! Tad was right. Jake had made a promise to teach him all he needed to know about selling. Looking back he had to admit that he hadn't kept his promise. He never once met with Tad to give him any pointers or help him improve his sales. Truth be told, he had been so wrapped up in his own life he had totally forgotten about that part of their agreement.

Looking at Tad with remorse, he said, "I hear what you are saying, Tad, and I am truly sorry. I'm glad you are bringing it up now. What can I do to make it up to you?"

"Well, all I'm still really asking for is some training," said Tad. "I'd like to come along with you or Bill on a few of your sales calls."

"That's a great idea," said Jake, "I'm sure we can arrange that." But Jake didn't feel satisfied with either Tad's request or his own reply. He realized that the request wasn't very clear and his reply was too vague. If he ended the conversation right there, as he normally did, most likely nothing would happen. They all would go their way and the whole thing would further hurt their relationship.

"Tad," Jake said, "to make an effective request, you need to give some context as to why you are making the request and specify who you would like to do what and by when. Could you make a specific request of either Bill or me that will get you what you want?"

"Bill," said Tad, feeling like he was in school, "Because my numbers are so bad and I would like to learn from you, will you take me on your sales calls for the next two weeks?"

"And do what?" Bill said to be silly and diffuse his discomfort with the situation.

"Allow me to witness how you close sales so that I can learn from you," Tad clarified.

"No problem, and if it's okay, I'd like to make a request of you," said Bill.

"Hold on, Bill," said Jake, "I haven't heard you actually accept the request."

"I said 'no problem,'" Bill cajoled. "Isn't that good enough?"

"Sometimes it is, and sometimes it isn't. Since we are emphasizing clarity right now and working on our fundamentals, I would prefer that you'd be really clear," Jake added.

Without hesitation, Bill answered like a pro, "Yes, I will take you along on my sales calls for the next two weeks, Tad. Happy?"

"That's good," Jake said. "Now go ahead with your request for Tad."

Bill spoke quickly: "Will you schedule four to six appointments for me this week?"

"Yes, I will," said Tad.

"Beautiful demonstration of requests and promises, guys," said Jake. "You may think that we are overdoing it, but I don't. We're just using a language that is very clear and leaves little room for misinterpretation. If you think it takes time to be clear up front, it's nothing compared to the time miscommunication takes. Now it's all about keeping the promises you made."

> **If you think it takes time to be clear up front, it's nothing compared to the time miscommunication takes.**

Then Jean chimed in, "Well, it sounds simple enough that we could talk like this all the time, and it sure would make things clearer. But it won't help me make more calls."

"Let's look at that," said Jake. "Maybe it will. What is it you need from us, Jean? Since you are feeling stressed, maybe you could make a request?"

After a few moments Jean's face came to life. "I've got it! Nathan, since you are not much into sales but very good at setting appointments, would you be willing to set up six or seven appointments a week for me starting this week?"

"I can't do it this week," replied Nathan, "but I will do it the following week, and the week after. Does that work for you?"

"That would be fine," said Jean, "thank you."

"Nice counter-offer, Nathan," said Jake. "I like the way you negotiated more time for yourself. Well done. Anyone else want to make a request or a promise?" Jake surveyed the table looking for another taker.

Everyone's eyes went to Crystal, who to this point hadn't said a word.

Crystal immediately leaned back in her chair and crossed her arms. Jake knew he couldn't be sure what Crystal was thinking, but it seemed a safe bet from her body language that she wasn't very happy.

Before Jake figured out how to approach Crystal, Tad, emboldened by the conversation so far, jumped in. "What do you think about all this, Crystal? Do you have any requests or promises you would like to make?"

"Frankly," Crystal began, "I'm on track to make the sales convention on my own, and so in answer to your question, no, I don't."

Jean covered her mouth to muffle her gasp, and the men in the room shot each other expectant glances. This was going to be good. Jake tapped his pen on the table in front of him for a moment to edit his thoughts and suppress his desire to take Crystal out at the knees. He knew this, like every moment, was an opportunity to enhance communication, and he decided to discuss her shortcomings as a teammate in private.

Jake looked up from the table and addressed Crystal directly. "I have no doubt that you will make it on your own. What you are doing works for you. My only request is that we meet for a half hour each week to review your sales to see if there is anything I can do to help you."

Crystal's face flushed as she realized how offensive her comment had been. "I'm sorry," she said quickly. "I didn't mean to be so negative. I guess I've got my doubts."

"That's fine," consoled Jake. "We're all challenged by this new approach, and as great as it is that we've upgraded the level of our communication, the key will be whether we all fulfill on our promises."

"Yes," said Crystal, "that's a better way of putting what I was thinking. And I accept your request."

As it became clear the meeting was nearly over, the team began reflecting on what had just happened. Privately they wondered if aliens had taken over Jake's body. What had happened to the Jake McKay who yelled at all of them just last week?

"Well," Jake said, "it looks like everyone has committed to a plan, and we all know exactly who will do what by when, except for Crystal and me. She and I need to set a time to get together. Let's do that right now, Crystal, and the rest of you can get to work."

Jake left the room feeling proud. This hadn't been comfortable for him, but it hadn't been that bad either. At points it was pretty exciting to hear the requests and promises stated so clearly. He had a strong sense his people would do what they said they would do.

Closing The Loop

"Coach," said Jake, "people don't do what they say they will do."

Three days had passed since the big staff meeting, and although there did seem to be a new attitude and people were taking action at a new level, Tad hadn't fulfilled his promise to get four appointments for Bill and in several other instances people didn't come through on their promises. Sometimes it was their own fault, sometimes something more important got in the way, and sometimes it was something beyond their control.

Jake wiped the sweat from his face with the front of his shirt as he sat himself down in the dugout for another coaching session. Little League practice had just ended, and Jake had thrown batting practice for a full hour. Coach handed him a bottle of water, grateful for not having to throw in the fierce humidity. Jake had left work early to allow ample time for practice and a conversation with Coach. He felt happy to have the distraction this afternoon because tonight he would call Christine.

"What would you like to learn today?" asked Coach.

"Well, your Integrity Tools diagram looks great on paper," said Jake, "but how do you maintain integrity in the real world? It seems most people try to do what they say, but things get in the way."

"As you might have guessed," said Coach, "there's more to the model than what we've covered so far. We'll finish the model today and give you some new tools. Also, the real world is always more complicated than what you see on paper. You know how in football they diagram plays using Xs and Os?"

"Sure," said Jake.

"On paper it looks like every play should go for a touchdown," Coach explained. "*These* Os block *these* Xs and the ball carrier runs through the hole for a touchdown. But it rarely works that way. Something breaks down and the runner gets tackled. In reality, *this* O blocking *this* X is actually two 300-pound lineman/warriors engaged in hand-to-hand combat. It's not neat and pretty like it looks on paper.

"With the Integrity Tools, the 300-pounders complicating things are people's emotions. Human emotion is not neat and pretty. But just as in football or baseball or anything else, if you know the fundamentals, and you

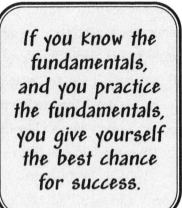

If you know the fundamentals, and you practice the fundamentals, you give yourself the best chance for success.

practice the fundamentals, you give yourself the best chance for success."

"I hear you," said Jake. "So what's the next step in the model?"

"Let me first say, Jake, that I acknowledge you for the changes you've made so far. You've really been willing to step outside of your comfort zone and be different, and you've done a terrific job on your homework. You've done what you promised."

"There's still a lot of work to do," said Jake, lips pressed tightly together, head shaking, "like with Jean..."

"Jake," interrupted Coach, "I just gave you an acknowledgement and you brushed it off. I'd like to point out something about that. An acknowledgement is like a gift, like a present you give someone on his or her birthday or anniversary. How would you feel if you wrapped a nice gift for Christine, and when you gave it to her she brushed it aside and left it sitting at the table where you gave it to her?"

"Not too good," said Jake.

"Right, and that's how I felt when you ignored my acknowledgement," Coach acknowledged.

"What should I have done?" asked Jake.

"Come on, Jake," said Coach, "what do you say when someone gives you a gift?"

"Thank you," Jake said demurely.

"That's right," said Coach, "but this isn't just about being polite. When someone acknowledges you, positive energy comes your way. I'm not sure how it works, but saying thank you lets that positive energy in. Too often people do what you just did – block the energy by ignoring or deflecting the acknowledgement so the energy is wasted. Even worse, the giver of the acknowledgment is apt to feel snubbed."

"Okay," said Jake somewhat impatiently. "Thank you. Now what is the next step in the model?"

"**Acknowledge** *is* the next step in the model," said Coach as he pulled out the diagram he had started days before. "It closes the integrity loop.

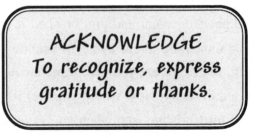

ACKNOWLEDGE
To recognize, express gratitude or thanks.

When you have a gap, make a request, get a promise and the person fulfills the promise, acknowledging them closes the loop. It completes the deal. Here again a simple thank you will do. Thank you tells the promisor that he or she has fulfilled the promise to your satisfaction.

"Perhaps more importantly," continued Coach, "acknowledging someone who has fulfilled a promise enhances the three areas affected by integrity:

1) It enhances **performance** since the person feels appreciated. It makes it more likely he or she will come through for you again next time.

2) It enhances **trust** between the people involved since it highlights an experience where the person was true to his or her word.

3) It enhances **personal power.** It helps the person who fulfilled the promise feel good about himself or herself."

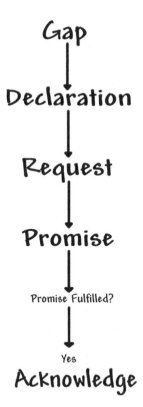

Gap

Declaration

Request

Promise

Promise Fulfilled?

Yes

Acknowledge

Jake looked up from his notebook where he had been furiously scribbling notes. "I'd always known acknowledging people was a nice thing to do, but now that you spell it out, I can see how important it is."

"Yes," said Coach, "and sadly people don't get much acknowledgement in most organizations. People are too busy, too reluctant to give others credit, and they don't know how to do it powerfully. But also most people typically just don't accept acknowledgements well. If you give people presents and they don't accept them, you'll soon stop giving them."

"Well, I know I don't get much acknowledgement, and what I do get I probably fight off," said Jake.

"How's that working for you?" asked Coach.

"Not well," admitted Jake.

"This is a vital topic," Coach continued, obviously passionate about this issue. "What people want most in life is to feel that they make a difference, that they matter. Too often they don't feel that way, especially in businesses. Upper management's perspective is often that salaries are enough of an acknowledgement, but that's not true. The research clearly shows that money is important

> **People function on emotional currency as much as they do monetary currency.**

to employees but not most important. People function on emotional currency as much as they do on monetary currency.

"Acknowledging people closes the integrity loop and cements it shut. It enhances subsequent performance, builds trust between the people involved, and makes both people feel good about themselves."

"I see," said Jake, still writing.

"But as you just demonstrated, it isn't easy for most people to fully accept an acknowledgement. It's a bit more emotional energy than their inner circuitry is used to. I think it's largely because the positive acknowledgement feels inconsistent with their self-image. But if you start letting acknowledgements in you get more comfortable with them. So let's try it again," Coach continued.

"Jake, you've done a great job of applying what you've learned. You do your homework and stretch yourself outside of your comfort zone."

"Thank you," said Jake after taking in a deep breath. It definitely felt different to voice the words. He had been so focused on what wasn't working that he had brushed off Coach's first acknowledgement unconsciously. It hadn't even registered. This time he felt a warmth and pride in his chest. It was uncomfortable, but good.

"Did you feel that?" asked Coach.

"Yes," said Jake.

"Me too," said Coach. "It feels good to me when someone accepts my gifts! So thank you for that."

"Thank *you*," said Jake.

They both enjoyed a quiet moment feeling good before Jake's male emotional circuitry was overloaded. He leaned forward quickly and blurted out, "So anyway, back to breaking promises…"

"Yes. Have you fulfilled all your promises this week?" asked Coach.

Crystalizing

A sudden insight caused Jake to miss Coach's question. For some time now Jake had been trying to figure out how to connect with Crystal. She was still producing, but good players make their teammates better. Crystal caused enough discord with her attitude that she actually made her teammates worse.

Perhaps Crystal needed acknowledgement. Thinking psychologically, since Crystal had lost her father at an early age she may actually be starving for acknowledgement. Her attitude suggested she didn't need it (she seemed to scoff at praise that came her way), but Jake had learned from his perception homework that people sometimes put on a front that hides their true feelings.

Jake had bought into her fierce self-sufficiency act and had stopped acknowledging her. He couldn't think of the last time he'd really praised her for her performance beyond a superficial, "good job." Granted, he was not a fan of Crystal and it was often the last thing he felt like doing for her, but he made a note to start looking for things, especially team-oriented things, that he could acknowledge her for.

Honoring Promises

"Um, I'm sorry Coach," said Jake, "what did you ask me?"

"Did you fulfill all your promises this week?"

"Most of them," said Jake, wanting to be proud of his improvement but troubled by his imperfection. "I think I did pretty much what I said I would, but I was later than I'd promised in a few cases."

"No one fulfills *all* of his or her promises," said Coach. "Life gets in the way and competing, higher priorities come up. But you can honor all of your promises. A way to honor your promise without fulfilling it is to **re-negotiate** it before you reach the deadline. As soon as you know the promise is in serious jeopardy, go to the person you made the promise to and do three things:

> *No one fulfills all their promises, but you can honor all your promises.*

1) Apologize.

2) Ask about the damages your re-negotiating might cause.

3) Work out the best solution possible in light of your new situation and make a new promise."

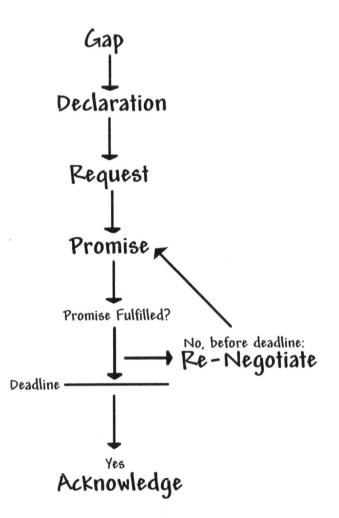

"Let me guess," said Jake, "the sooner you re-negotiate your promise after you realize you likely won't fulfill it, the better it will be for your performance, the trust in the relationship, and your personal power."

"You've got it," said Coach.

"That seems pretty straightforward," said Jake.

"Again, common sense is not common practice," said Coach. "For various reasons people often don't re-negotiate promises."

"True," said Jake. "Why is that?"

"The usual suspects," said Coach, "fear - not wanting to look bad or seem incompetent. Also, often people don't take giving their word seriously so they don't think it will matter if they miss a deadline."

"Yes, it often takes all the courage I can muster to admit I'm not going to fulfill a promise," said Jake, "but it's better than making a big mess of things."

"Exactly," said Coach, "and that's the next step in the model and a second way to honor your promises: **Clean up a mess.** If you didn't fulfill a promise and you didn't re-negotiate before the deadline, your integrity circle gapes wide open. Your performance, trust and personal power leak out all over the place. In order to restore integrity you need to clean up your mess.

"Cleaning up a mess is much like re-negotiating, it just comes after the original promise deadline instead of before it. When you realize you've broken a promise and want to get back into integrity, contact the person you made the promise to and do three things:

1. Admit that you didn't fulfill the promise and apologize appropriately.

2. Ask about how your failure to fulfill the promise affected the other person and make amends as needed.

3. Make a new promise."

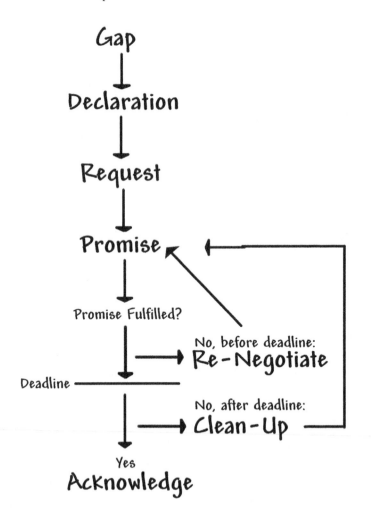

"That sounds simple enough," said Jake, "but my pride and ego make it pretty tough sometimes to fess-up and re-negotiate a promise, much less clean up when I break a promise."

"All of these steps can be difficult," said Coach, "operating in integrity takes courage. But it's one of life's many paradoxes. If you do the hard things, life is easy. If you only do the easy things, life is hard."

> *If you do the hard things, life is easy. If you only do the easy things, life is hard.*

Jake took a long slow breath and sent a distant stare out over the playing field. He certainly had integrity messes with Christine and would clean up his act with her tonight. (He checked his watch – still plenty of time before *the call.*) There were more messes at the office for sure. Thinking of his staff prompted a situation that didn't seem to fit in the model.

"What do I do when someone has made a promise to me," said Jake, "and the deadline has passed, and they haven't fulfilled the promise, re-negotiated *or* cleaned up their mess?"

"**Complain!**" said Coach.

"Great!" exclaimed Jake, "I was hoping you'd say that. I'm pretty good at complaining."

"Well...,"
began Coach.

Jake inter-
rupted, "I expect
you've got some
rules to follow in
order to do it
with integrity."

> ## COMPLAIN
> A process followed by the receiver of a promise to restore integrity when the promise has been broken.

"Indeed," said Coach. "Complaining is the last Integrity Tool of the model because it draws on all of the other tools. It has three rules up front, then a pretty detailed procedure to follow. I think it is the most involved tool because you're often dealing with the most emotion. Both parties can have their juices flowing. But don't worry about getting it exactly right. If you control your own emotions and are respectful, the actual steps are pretty intuitive."

"Bring it on," said Jake, pen and notebook ready.

"The first rule is that you can complain only if you originally got a promise. You can't complain to one of your staff about not completing a report if he or she didn't promise to do it. The same goes for complaining to your boss for treating you a certain way if he didn't promise he wouldn't treat you that way."

> **You can only complain if you originally got a promise.**

"Good one," said Jake. "That ups the ante even more for being clear up front on the promise."

"Yes," said Coach, "otherwise you have no traction later on. Think of a promise as a contract. If there are any disputes later on, you go back and check what the contract actually says. If a promise wasn't clear up front, you can't expect clarity or satisfaction later."

"I see," said Jake.

"From a broader perspective," said Coach taking a deep breath, "as a culture, we tend to expect things from the world with a sense of entitlement instead of taking personal responsibility for asking for or earning them. Rather than making requests, which puts you at risk of hearing no, you assume they said yes and crucify them for not complying!"

"I think that's pretty common in most offices," said Jake.

"Yes, you expect things to be different. You think they should change, but no one actually promised you they would. With no promise, you don't have a valid complaint. It is entirely appropriate, however, for you to request what you want."

"There's more integrity in that," Jake offered.

"One of the main goals of using the Integrity Tools is to create a work environment based on the word and integrity of individuals instead of their unspoken personal expectations," said Coach.

"Powerful stuff," said Jake.

"Yes, and it gets better," said Coach. "The second rule of complaining is that you only complain to someone who can do something about your issue. Typically people talk to co-workers about what the boss did or didn't do or about what someone in another work group promised to do but didn't. That isn't complaining as I define it, it's whining or gossiping.

> **The second rule of complaining is that you only complain to someone who can do something about your issue.**

Show me a company where people whine to each other about what so-and-so did when so-and-so isn't in the room, and I'll show you a company that under-performs, lacks trust, and is full of disempowered people. If you are upset about someone or some policy or some work condition, complain to a person who can do something about it or keep it to yourself."

"What is everyone going to talk about at the water cooler if they buy into this rule?" asked Jake.

"How to do their jobs better," said Coach, smiling as he completed the diagram.

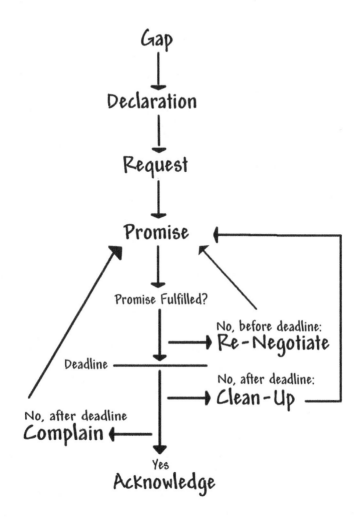

"The third rule of complaining is to only complain when you feel centered or level headed. As you learned in your days as a pitcher, your performance suffers if you lose your cool. If you're angry and upset, the conversation has a high likelihood of creating the opposite effect you want it

> **The third rule of complaining is to only complain when you are feeling centered or level headed.**

to. It might feel good to blow your top at someone, but the other person will feel attacked and get defensive. You can't say a constructive thing when you are in a destructive emotion."

"I can see that," said Jake, remembering the meeting where he was in the "wrong" emotion and blasted his staff.

"If you follow the process I'll give you," said Coach, "you have a good chance of increasing the trust between

> **You can't say a constructive thing when you are in a destructive emotion.**

you and your colleagues instead of decreasing it."

"Then," said Jake, "assuming I got a promise from a person, I'm speaking to that individual, and I have blown off my steam before I sit down with him: How do I complain without alienating him? I'm often afraid to confront people when they haven't fulfilled their promises because I feel that if I attack them, our relationship will suffer."

"Yes, but it is going to suffer worse if you don't say anything. In fact, you are out of integrity if you don't bring it up – you're failing to honor the promise that was made. The issue will sit there for you as an open loop undermining your energy and trust with the person until it gets addressed."

"I hear you," said Jake.

Coach reached into his bag, pulled out a one-page summary of how to complain effectively and gave it to Jake. It was essentially a script Jake could use that emphasized dealing with the facts of the situation to neutralize the confounding effects of emotion.

Coach continued, "You might also add a request such as, 'If for any reason you realize you won't be able to fulfill your promise on time, would you please let me know as soon as possible?'"

Key elements for complaining effectively include:

1. Set a context for the conversation by asking the person if he or she has time to talk right then.
2. Check your facts. Ask if the person understood the promise the same way you did.
3. Ask for an explanation, e.g., ask about what happened.
4. Tell the person what damage his or her failure to fulfill the promise caused you.
5. Make a new request based on the new current circumstances.
6. Request a new promise.

"Good one," said Jake.

"Hopefully it's obvious to you that you break away from this script any time common sense suggests it," Coach added. "It might take seconds to go through this; it might take hours. You can't force the guy to apologize. You can't make him do anything for that matter."

"But it sounds like this would give me a good chance to get my point across and move the guy into action without being overly confrontational," Jake said.

"It helps you be powerful without being forceful. You don't back down, and you don't try to overwhelm the person with emotion or leverage," Coach explained in his wise and confident way.

"It seems respectful, too," added Jake.

Pointing at the script Coach prophesized, "At some point in the not-too-distant future you will hear someone violate one of the three rules about complaining, and you'll have a chance to teach this to him or her. I'm no psychic, but I've been around humans long enough to know that if you aren't hearing some misdirected belly-aching right now, it's on the way."

"I have no complaints about today," smiled Jake. "This was great. Now it's just a matter of putting these tools into action."

"Yes," said Coach lifting that bushy eyebrow, "and listen carefully to this final piece...."

The Be Attitudes

Coach leaned toward Jake to make sure Jake got the impact of his words. "Don't fall into the trap of thinking that complaining, or any Integrity Tool, is about the exact words you say. The words themselves are not magical; they are not even what is most important. The words I've suggested to you are the *text* for what to

> **The words themselves are not magical; how you say something creates the context for the communication.**

say, but how you say the words creates the *context* for the communication, which is much more important. That's why I said at the beginning, if you keep your emotions in check and stay respectful, you'll do well.

"Remember that we started your coaching talking about your perspective of your staff and choosing to be a **player** instead of a **victim**?"

"Certainly."

"We then emphasized your being in integrity yourself, and only then got into the Integrity Tools. We did it in that order because how you are *being* is more important than what you say. Be a player. Be authentic. Be caring. Be

> Be a player. Be authentic. Be caring. Be respectful. And be powerful without being forceful. Then use the Integrity Tools, and you will have done everything you can to produce the result you want.

respectful. And be powerful without being forceful. Then use the Integrity Tools, and you will have done everything you can to produce the results you want," Coach summarized.

Jake drew a deep breath and slowly let it out. He knew Coach was on the money. Everything he had heard from Coach – the Integrity Tools and now the importance of how he was being as compared to what words he was saying, resonated as true. He just could never have articulated it the way Coach had. Jake knew the ball was now in his court to make this a way of life.

"Just remember," said Coach, "that the Integrity Tools are skills, and as such, you and your team develop them with practice. Also, like a diagram of a football play, it looks good on paper but is a lot more challenging in real life."

Jake nodded.

"So, Jake," Coach, asked, "did you get an answer to your original question on how you can maintain integrity in the real world?"

"Very much so," said Jake. "One huge concept is that I can't fulfill all my promises, but I can maintain integrity by honoring all my promises. If I know before a deadline that I won't reach it, I need to call the person I made a promise to and re-negotiate. If I totally blew it and missed a deadline, use the three-step clean-up process. And if someone breaks a promise to me – or at least I think it was broken..."

"Nice catch," laughed Coach.

"...then I check the facts, get an explanation and, hopefully, an apology (although I can't control that), and a new promise. The key piece about complaining, and the rest of the Integrity Tools, hinges on being authentic, respectful and powerful without being forceful."

"Yes," acknowledged Coach. "And the best way for you to learn this stuff is to share it with others. Your homework is to use these tools and teach them to your staff. The process of explaining deepens your understanding, plus then they can hold you accountable for operating this way."

"Will do," said Jake. "I'm grateful for all that you've done for me. Thank you."

"You're welcome," said Coach humbly, letting the acknowledgement sink in.

Buoyed by his conversation with Coach and excited and nervous about the upcoming phone call, Jake hustled across the field to his car to drive home.

He had plenty of time before his appointment to call Christine, but he didn't want to take any chances on calling her late. He wanted to be home, showered, and feeling fresh when he called.

PART FOUR

Upgrading

Hitting Home

"Hi Christine, how are you?" said Jake.

Silence.

"Hello, Christine, what's going on?" said Jake, a bit more suave.

More silence.

"Hey Chris, what's shakin'?"

That definitely wasn't it.

Jake was practicing. He wanted his words to sound confident and trustworthy when he called her, but also loving and emotionally available.

Fortunately, as the minutes ticked down toward the time for the call, something Coach said revisited Jake's brain, "How you are being is more important than what you say." Jake decided he would just be himself. He coached himself: "Be authentic and loving, and trust that I'll know what to say." He remembered his last tele-

> **How you are being is more important than what you say.**

phone conversation with Christine and recognized that he came on too strong. This time he wanted to listen more.

As the clock struck seven he anxiously dialed her number. He felt something move in his chest when she answered the phone.

"Hi, Christine, it's great to hear your voice. How are things going?"

Christine chatted briefly, filling the nervous energy between them with trivia.

"How are things going for you?" she asked.

"Except for missing you, things are going really well. I'm learning so much, and I want to share it with you. I see so much more clearly how I've let you down. There is no way you could trust me the way I have operated with you."

That one hit home with Christine. Something seemed different about Jake. She wondered: *Has he changed or is it just that I so much want him to?*

"Could I come over and talk with you?" said Jake, wanting to be Mr. Powerful Integrity Man, but sounding more like pleading.

"Yes," said Christine "Come by at eight o'clock."

Pitching To Christine

Christine lived just off of Wisconsin Avenue, about a mile north of Georgetown. Stopping and going through the many northbound traffic lights on Wisconsin, Jake noticed a small flower shop closing for the evening. In an instant he pulled into an open parking space (that was his perception anyway, it was actually a no parking area) and carefully picked out the right bouquet of pink roses, Christine's favorite.

Five minutes early and flowers in hand, Jake knocked on her door. She answered wearing an old pair of sweatpants and a T-shirt, her hair tied in a ponytail. The first thought in Jake's head was that she was the most beautiful woman he had ever seen.

"Hi," Christine said. "Come on in."

Jake nervously entered her neat apartment and handed her the flowers. As she took them to the kitchen to put them in water, Jake took a deep breath and slowly exhaled as he sat on the couch. Coach had taught him during his playing days in high school to take a deep breath on the mound before each pitch; he'd found it helped him stay in control and trust his ability in pressure situations. It came in handy now as he prepared to make one of the biggest pitches of his life.

Christine carried the flowers in a vase to the coffee table in front of Jake and placed them carefully on the table. Short-circuiting trivial pleasantries, Jake reached for her hand and motioned for her to sit down beside him.

"I've been a fool," Jake began. "You have been right all along."

"That's a good start," she said, lightly lifting her ebony eyebrows and nodding her head, "go on."

He told her about his revelations of how his perception (his inner Oakleys), had limited his staff, and how horrible it felt when he got in touch with the effects of his lack of integrity. He shared about his declaration to the team and talked her briefly through the Integrity Tools.

It was obvious to Christine that Jake felt embarrassed by his previous actions, and she was encouraged that he had recognized the problem. Christine sensed that he had a genuine need and desire to change.

"Chris," Jake said, "as poorly as I've communicated with my staff, I realize I've been worse with you. You were right in what you said at *Taverna* that night. I've never told you how I feel about you. I've never declared my intentions with you."

Jake adjusted his position on the couch and cleared his throat. Squeezing her hand, he looked her in the eyes and said, "I love you."

Jake continued as he saw tears well in her eyes. "Just like you said, I haven't shown you that I'm a man of integrity. I repeatedly broke promises I made to you. I want you to know I'm changing my ways and intend to prove to you that I can be a man of my word. I'm working on becoming the kind of man you would want to spend the rest of your life with."

"And how would you know what kind of man that is?" she asked playfully.

"I don't know exactly, but I am sure you'll let me know," he replied as they shared a tension-relieving laugh.

She turned to him and said with a serious voice, "I want to have a future with you too, but I don't want any more empty promises, Jake."

"No more empty promises. I promise," he responded.

Cristine put her hand comfortably on his leg, the way she always used to. As she began filling him in on what had been happening at the hospital, Jake had an idea.

"Are you up for some Lebanese food?" he said. "I'd like another chance to at least make it to the part where we order our meals."

"Let's go," said Christine.

Something To Complain About

Momentum also had shifted at the office. The team still had a long way to go to fulfill on Jake's declaration, and they had even less time to achieve their goals, but the changes Jake made in the way he operated correlated with a significant boost in sales by the staff.

Jean had created a chart shaped like a thermometer to function as a scoreboard for their progress toward the convention. Nathan's idea of calling existing clients to discuss expanding or adding policies worked as well as they'd hoped. Many of the clients seemed to actually appreciate the phone call because they hadn't thought about how their needs had changed.

A sorely lacking camaraderie was steadily building, but Coach was right in his prediction that before long one of them would come to him to complain about another. Tad sat across from Jake.

"Have you talked to Bill about this?" asked Jake.

"Not really," said Tad.

"Not really?" said Jake. "Then why are you talking to me about it? Your beef is with him, so you need to talk with him."

"What am I going to say?" asked Tad, obviously uncomfortable with the idea. "The guy is centuries older than I am, and has sold more policies than I can dream of. I thought he was on my side, but it turns out he's a jerk."

"That's one possible perspective, but it sounds like fiction to me. Did he make you a promise?" asked Jake.

"Yes," said Tad. "He said he would give me a percentage of the sales we did together last week, and I don't see that anywhere in the paperwork he's turned in."

"Then it doesn't matter how much experience he has," said Jake. "You have the right, and the obligation, to complain to him. I'm certainly not going to talk with him for you; you'll have to sort it out with him yourself. Then if you can't resolve it with him, invite him to come with you to see me. If he won't come with you, tell him you are coming to me to talk about it. That's the way we do it around here. There's no integrity in your just coming straight to me."

Tad sat silently for a few moments, and then said, "If I don't talk to him, I'll lose out on the commissions and resent him for as long as I live. But if I do say something, he might blow a gasket and stop teaching me his sales techniques."

"I can give you some coaching on having that conversation," said Jake.

"That would be cool," replied Tad.

"What would you like to have happen?" said Jake, taking a page out of Coach's playbook.

"I'd like Bill to make good on his promise to pay me 25 percent of his commission on the policies we sold last week," Tad explained.

Jake pulled out the sheet Coach had given him on complaining and went over the three rules: Only complain if you received a promise; only talk to someone who can do something about your complaint; and only talk if you are in control of yourself emotionally.

With Jake playing Bill's role, they role-played Tad's conversation with Bill multiple times. Each time, Jake coached Tad on how he could present his case skillfully and powerfully to Bill without being forceful. Tad used the script sheet at first, but as he got more comfortable with the process, he ad-libbed.

The key piece Tad needed to remember was to start by checking the facts of the promise, making sure that he and Bill understood the promise in the same way. If Bill did agree he had made that promise to Tad, Tad would simply ask Bill why he hadn't complied with the request.

> **Start by checking the facts of the promise, making sure that all parties understand the promise in the same way.**

And if they reached that point without resolution, Tad would make a new request. Before long, Tad felt confident.

Jake asked Tad what he had learned from the coaching. Tad explained, "First, that Bill might not be a jerk, and second that I can raise this issue with Bill in a way that isn't a Battle Royal confrontation. I can actually see this going pretty well."

"Great job," said Jake, "and by when will you have this conversation with Bill?"

"By close of business tomorrow," said Tad.

"Go for it."

"Thanks, Jake," said Tad as he left Jake's office. "All managers should be as good a coach as you."

"Thank you, Tad," said Jake, enjoying the buzz of accepting the acknowledgement. *And thank you, Coach,* Jake said to himself.

Things Get "Rocky"

Three months after their first conversation, Jake called Coach exactly at the time they had agreed upon eleven days before. "Coach," Jake said excitedly into the phone, "you know in the first Rocky movie where Rocky is training for the big fight with Apollo Creed and that great theme music is playing?" asked Jake.

"Yes," Coach said as he recognized the scene.

"Where Rocky is in his gray sweats and he's running early in the morning, doing one-handed push-ups, eating raw eggs..."

"Yes, I know it, Jake."

"And carrying that big wooden thing, and punching raw meat in the freezer..."

"Yes, Jake!" interrupted Coach, "and if you don't get to the point I'm going to come over and punch *you*."

"I feel like that scene is going on here," said Jake.

"Did you issue everyone gray sweats?" said Coach.

"No," laughed Jake, happy to now enjoy Coach's humor, "but things are going really well these past few weeks. The tools, language, model and everything are getting easier for me, more natural, and the staff is really picking up on it. We have our breakdowns, but we've officially upgraded our interpersonal operating system."

"That's great, Jake," said Coach, his smile evident through the phone. "Congratulations. It isn't easy to change people's behavior. Their use of the tools is a nice acknowledgement of you."

"Thank you," said Jake, taking a moment to appreciate Coach's praise.

"How are you helping them learn the distinctions of the model?"

"The big thing is that I'm doing the best I can to follow the model myself. I can't hold them to a standard I'm not holding myself to. I've also explained the model in staff meetings and requested they use it in their interactions with each other and our customers. I often pull the diagram out during one-on-one conversations to help determine where communication breakdowns happen."

> *The big thing is that I'm doing the best I can to follow the model myself. I can't hold others to a standard I'm not holding myself to.*

"Sounds good, Jake," said Coach. "Now give me some examples. What kind of things do you see and hear that make you think they really use it?"

"Well," said Jake, "you were right about how someone would complain to me about someone else. I held my ground with Tad when he came in whining about an issue with Bill. I taught him the complaining rules and process, and he had the conversation with Bill he had feared. Tad said it helped him to go in with a respectful, but powerful approach. It worked out great.

"Turns out Bill understood the original promise differently and didn't think he was out of integrity with Tad. Tad felt great about it. In your terms he gained a lot of personal power, and they've worked well together since then."

"Way to go, Jake! That's good coaching."

"Thanks," said Jake. "I had a significant change of lenses in how I see Crystal. I shifted from perceiving her as a difficult person for me to get along with to seeing her as a person whose edge is simply a way to protect her from getting hurt. I've asked myself, 'How does she help the team?' and acknowledged her for what I've seen instead of just looking through my Crystal-is-a-problem lenses. I can't say it's been miraculous, but I know I'm slowly winning her respect and I can see her edge dulling. She even volunteered the other day to explain something to Tad. Believe me, for Crystal that is a big step. I've also noticed it's less stressful for me to look for the positive in her than to carry a grudge."

"Very nice," said Coach.

> I've also noticed it's less stressful for me to look for the positive in someone than to carry a grudge.

"I also know the model is into my staff's daily operations because I hear the vocabulary in their interactions. I hear words like promise, request, integrity, counter-offer, and clean up in their hallway exchanges. Just yesterday I even heard Jean say, 'I need to clean something up with you,' to Crystal. That never would have happened before."

"Great," smiled Coach.

"I must say Jean and her emotional soup are still quite a mystery to me," added Jake. "I think her improved performance is mostly a matter of a rising tide lifting all ships. As everyone else has stepped up she's been more focused, sort of like peer pressure. The rest of the team won't tolerate her whining so I haven't had to deal with it much."

"That happens when you create a culture of integrity."

"And I cracked up the other day when I heard Bill talking to a customer on the phone about how he holds a promise he makes verbally to the same standard he would a written policy. And then he said 'I promise you'll have the pricing for your policy by 10:30 tomorrow morning.'"

"Touché," laughed Coach.

"They have become pretty relentless with this 'who will do what by when' bit. It's as if an epidemic of 'by when' has broken out. Anytime someone tells someone else they will do something, the other person says 'by when?'"

Jake was rolling now as he and Coach shared more laughter. Coach could hear the pride in Jake's voice as he continued: "I've had to give almost all of my staff your little talk on receiving acknowledgements. I've been dishing them out much more liberally than I had previously, and I see that people don't typically really let the positive energy in."

"Yes," said Coach, "isn't that interesting how people seem to defend themselves against compliments? Be sure as you acknowledge people that you tell them specifically what you like about what they did. For example, 'Great job turning that Dorigan report out in less than 30 minutes' shapes the person's behavior better than simply, 'Great job.'"

"Will do," said Jake, jotting the coaching point in his notebook. "Oh, and by the way," he added coyly, "the sales numbers are up sharply. I think they have started to believe they can pull this off."

"It sounds really good, Jake," said Coach, "Keep doing what you're doing."

Keep doing what I am doing, Jake thought to himself as he hung up the phone. *That's nice to hear.*

Working (Things) Out With Christine

Christine and Jake now communicated better than ever. Yes, there were times when a crisis would occur at work and take priority over a promise he had made to her to have dinner or go to the movies, but he now called her as soon as he realized he couldn't keep his promise and re-negotiated. Christine finally felt Jake respected her time and his commitments to her, and she began to really feel appreciated. The more time they spent together, the more they talked and the more their relationship grew.

They even worked out together consistently. Three times a week, whether he felt like it or not, Jake met Christine at the gym for an hour. The key to his success was simply to schedule the workouts on his calendar and treat them like appointments with clients. This practice helped him in three now familiar areas:

1. His **performance**:

He had more and better energy all through the day. This made everything easier, especially the administrative part of his job, which he hated.

2. The **trust** between Christine and him:

    Jake's credibility with Christine rose sharply as his recent reliability gradually overshadowed his past failings.

3. His own **personal power**:

    It just plain felt good to know that his word meant something. Instead of integrity messes draining his energy and forcing him into scramble mode, Jake had a strong sense he could create whatever he wanted in his life. The passing weeks only convinced him further that he wanted to include Christine in his future life.

"Trust is built over time just like muscle," Jake remembered Coach saying in one of their conversations. "Each promise you make and keep is like a repetition with a barbell.

> **Trust is built over time just like muscle.**

One or two repetitions might feel good but won't change your physique much. But lots of reps over lots of time can create significant growth and strength to your muscles."

Jake could tell keeping his word with Christine was growing and strengthening their relationship.

On Success And Satisfaction

One day in late August Jake arranged for Christine to stop by the ball field where Coach, Jake and the team were practicing. Christine and Coach had heard a lot about each other, but Jake wanted these two important people in his life to meet.

She arrived just as Coach dismissed his Little League team, and Jake immediately grabbed her hand and eagerly led her toward Coach.

"Coach, I'd like you to meet Christine."

Christine smiled and held out her hand as Coach did the same. "So you're the lady who has captured Jake's heart," he said.

"I hope so," she replied. "And you're the gentleman who has taught Jake so much this summer, and for that I thank you from the bottom of my heart."

"You're very welcome," Coach beamed. "He's really done a nice job with things. Anyone can talk the talk, but not many walk the walk. I'd say overall you found yourself a pretty good man here."

"I agree," said Christine as she wrapped her arm around Jake and gave him a squeeze and a smile.

Coach and Christine quizzed each other on the get-to-know-you basics and chit-chatted about the pros and cons of living in the D.C. area. They even realized they had a mutual acquaintance.

"And what's the latest from the office?" Coach asked, turning his attention to Jake. "Are you guys going to qualify for the convention?"

"We're making a good run at it," said Jake. "It'll at least be close. We'll have to catch a few breaks, but no matter what happens I'm extremely proud of the way they've turned things around."

"That brings up a really important point that's tough for most people to get," said Coach. "Everyone focuses so much on results, but actually your results are outside of your control.

"For example, you can't make someone buy insurance from you. Just like a hitter can do everything right but have the shortstop catch his line drive, you can do a great job of selling your products to potential customers and still have them choose some other provider."

"That's for sure," said Jake. "It's one of the frustrating parts of my job."

"Yes, you don't actually control your own results," said Coach. "You don't control whether or not you reach your target numbers."

"I don't like to think that way, but it's certainly true," Jake agreed.

"Jot this one down," said Coach. "Success, as people often define it, is when your results are equal to or better than your goals. But since you can't control your results, you're in trouble if your happiness depends on the outcome of your efforts.

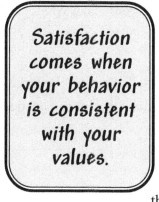

Success, as people often define it, is when your results are equal to, or better than your goals.

"So here's a second formula: Satisfaction, or peace, comes when your behavior is consistent with your values."

Satisfaction comes when your behavior is consistent with your values.

At Jake's request, Coach repeated the two ideas as Jake recorded them in his notebook.

Coach continued, "This idea of results being out of your control is no excuse for not giving your absolute best. For most people, excellence is one of their values. If you don't play full out to win, your behavior does not equal your values."

"I like that, Coach," said Jake, "It describes how I feel heading into this last month at work. Our team clearly has a value of working hard to achieve our goal, and their behavior has certainly been consistent with that value."

"That's a very satisfying feeling," said Coach.

"Coach," said Christine, shifting the focus, "how have your little sluggers made out this summer?"

"Terrific!" smiled Coach. "They've learned a lot and are having a lot of fun. I'm really proud of the way they've played."

"And of the way you coached, I presume," added Jake.

"Yes, I feel good about the perspective I've taken and the way I've worked with them," Coach acknowledged.

"Sounds like you're on your way to a championship season," said Christine.

"Actually, we've only won four games, so we won't even make the play-offs. Attitude can only take you so far. You need talent to actually win a lot of games," Coach expanded.

"I see," said Christine, backpedaling a bit. "Well, then I'm glad you all will walk away with a sense of satisfaction and peace over your behavior."

"She's a fast learner, Jake," chuckled Coach.

"That she is," Jake beamed.

"I hope your team makes their numbers, Jake," said Coach. "Sounds like they deserve it."

"They do," said Jake, "but I don't know where the team would be without your help. I certainly don't want to think about where *I* would be without your coaching. My life would be quite a bit different if I hadn't stopped by the field that day."

After setting their next meeting time, Jake made the familiar walk across the playing field, this time with Christine on his arm.

Christine commented on how nice a man she thought Coach was, but Jake didn't hear her; he was deep in thought: *I guess the same idea about getting the results you want holds true for a request as well: you can ask a woman to marry you, but you can't control what she says.*

Bottom Of The Ninth

On October 4th, Jake, Bill, Jean, Tad, Crystal and Nathan milled around the conference room sipping coffee and chit-chatting. Five months ago, at the infamous "Hurricane Jake" meeting, the tension in the room was around how badly they were going to be blown away by the rookie manager. Today the tension was quite different. They knew they had done great, they just weren't sure if they had done great enough.

September had been wild as they realized they could reach their goal and everyone caught convention fever. The staff felt as if they had landed on the set of the Jerry Lewis Telethon for Muscular Dystrophy as the numbers went up on the big board and the time ticked by.

Even at a hectic pace, they had operated in integrity as well as any business team could (well, at least for the last three months – those first three had been shaky). Now they waited to hear if their efforts had produced their desired results.

Jake had already given his no-matter-what-happens-I'm-proud-of-you-guys speech. He told them about Coach and his Little League team and even hung a picture of them on the wall near the water cooler. The boys' faces glowed with fun and the pride of having given their best all summer.

But right now each member of Jake's team wondered: Would we be like Coach's team, heads high with pride over our effort but no trip to the big dance? Or would it be satisfaction plus jubilation and a free trip to the Big Apple?

Then they all heard it, the sound that silenced the room. The fax machine rang and picked up. Jake set his coffee cup down on the credenza he was leaning against, and walked slowly over to the fax machine. He waited patiently for the pages to print, and when the machine finally stopped, he gathered them and eyed them carefully.

What took only seconds seemed like minutes until Jake finally raised his eyes from the paperwork and re-focused on the group. "The results are in from the home office about who qualified for the national sales convention," Jake announced and continued the suspense.

You could have heard a pin drop in the room as everyone held their breath and waited to hear the final numbers.

"It appears that our final qualifying premium figures were very close to the necessary amounts needed to make convention this year." Looks of disappointment started to cross several faces until Jake declared, "but we *exceeded* the minimum required! We made it: We're all going to the national sales convention in New York City next month!"

Hoots of happiness echoed throughout the room and everyone hugged and congratulated each other, celebrating as if they'd won the World Series. A few minutes later the phone rang, and Jake went to answer it back in his office away from the noise.

"Hey, Jake. Chuck Helfer here, at the home office. I just wanted to congratulate you and your team on the tremendous job you all did. I was right all along about you. You are as good a regional manager as you were a sales rep. In fact, I don't know if you realize this or not, but your small district office ended up being in the top nine percent of all our district offices – including ones much larger than yours. Great job, Jake. Well done."

Jake was grinning so wide it was hard to get his thank you out.

Popping

The party that night was at Jean's home. A few spouses plus Christine were there, but Bill, Jean, Crystal, Tad, Nathan and Jake ("The Team," as they had come to refer to themselves) were center stage. It was one of those all-too-rare times when every joke someone made got a laugh. No pretense, no concerns about what other people thought, they all just enjoyed being winners.

Jake had a permanent smile on his face and alternated between being fully present in the party moment and pulling back to reflect on what they had accomplished over the past six months. It was great in years past to qualify for convention as an individual rep, but it was much sweeter to share it with his whole team.

His call to Coach earlier had been fun, and he was looking forward to taking Coach to dinner to thank him more formally. They had reminisced about their first conversation when Jake was convinced his staff was a bunch of lazy losers and how Jake's choosing to change that perspective opened the door to a whole new possibility.

They also had swapped stories of Jake's adventures in learning to operate in integrity and then getting his staff on board with the Integrity Tools. Finally, they agreed that the bonus checks and the upcoming trip to the convention in

New York were nice, but seeing the staff set their interpersonal standards high and live up to them was the real victory.

At one point later in the evening, the whole team was hanging around the dining room area when Christine ran out to her car to bring in the special cake she had ordered. Although they didn't know Christine well, the team had certainly seen enough of her to like her and know that Jake was serious about her. They used Christine's absence as a chance to teasingly request that Jake share any declarations he had to make about their relationship.

His face aglow like a Little Leaguer who just hit his first home run, Jake waffled, then stepped up to the plate and said, "I'm going to ask her to marry me."

"Oh, yeah?" the team laughed in chorus, "by when?"

Get On The Field!

We hope you enjoyed reading *Who Will Do What By When?* But more importantly, we want it to spark upgrades to your performance, relationships, and personal power.

Reading this book is like us having a conversation in the dugout: It's a nice experience; but to really learn how to play, you have to get on the field and practice!

If you are ready to get on the field, get our free "Getting Started" guide and newsletter at :

www.HeadsUpPerformance.com

We'll periodically send you tips for implementing performance enhancing ideas that will help you stay on course (plus an occasional update on how Jake and Christine are doing).

Ready To Upgrade Your Performance?

Our seminars are customized to meet the specific business needs of clients. Often requested programs include:

Who Will Do What By When? **Success System™**

Like upgrading a computer's operating system, this program enhances a team's reliability, capacity and speed. Their new "interpersonal" operating system provides a platform for sustained excellence. A variety of formats are available.

At Your Best: The Fundamentals of Personal Performance

Athletes talk about being "in the zone" – a special mindset in which they are focused, confident and produce their best results. The same phenomenon happens in business. This program is based on the practices of world class athletes, executives, and other performers and empowers business people to be at their best on a consistent basis.

Evoking Excellence: Coaching Skills for Leaders

The most important variable in the performance and retention of talent in an organization is the relationship between an employee and his or her immediate supervisor. This program teaches managers and other leaders coaching skills that enable them to evoke excellence in their staff.

Personal Coaching

Would you like to have Coach on your team? Personal coaching provides an unmatched opportunity for performance improvement and personal growth. Regardless of current performance level, coaching provides the challenge, accountability, structure and outside perspective needed to become your best.

Who Will Sell What By When?

Many salespeople's entire plan consists of merely showing up, making a presentation, perhaps dealing with some objections, and hoping for the best. While winging it in this fashion will get them some sales, it's unlikely to make them rich. In this program we train participants to improve the odds of getting and keeping control of the sales process.

Past Clients Include:

The New York Yankees, Microsoft, MBIA, Kaiser
Permanente, The Corporate Finance Institute, Sylvan
Learning Company, Tampa Electric Company,
University Area Community Development Center, the
Virginia and Florida Departments of Transportation,
the Texas Rangers, and many individuals and work
groups from companies such as Nationwide Insurance,
Merrill Lynch, and Smith Barney.

**For more information about the authors and
their availability for presenting keynotes and
workshops, please contact them at:**

Tom Hanson, Ph.D.
813-968-8863
Tom@HeadsUpPerformance.com

Birgit Zacher Hanson, M.S.
813-963-6224
BZH@HeadsUpPerformance.com

Integrity Tools Vocabulary

Acknowledge: An expression of thankfulness and appreciation. The "final act" in any effective interpersonal exchange is the declaration of gratitude; for example, "Thank you." Declaring gratitude closes the loop opened by the original request or promise.

Cleaning up: Restoring integrity after a broken promise. The three-step clean up:

1. Acknowledge to the promisee that you (the promisor) didn't fulfill the promise. Apologize as appropriate.
2. Ask how your not fulfilling the promise affected the promisee and make amends as needed.
3. Make a new promise.

Complaint: An expression of grievance regarding an unfulfilled promise made to you with the intent of forwarding action on the task and restoring integrity to the relationship.

The three rules of complaining:

1. Only complain if you originally got a promise.
2. Only complain to the person who can do something to rectify your complaint (usually it's the one who gave you the promise).

3. Only complain when you are feeling centered or level headed.

When you've identified the proper person to complain to,
1. Check your facts:

"You promised me X, do you agree?"

"You haven't done X, true?"
2. If your facts are correct, express the cost to you that the promise was not fulfilled.
3. Make a request: "I now request that you do X (or an alternative)."

If you didn't get a *promise*, you don't have a *complaint*! You need to either make a *request* or forget about it!

Counter Offer: A proposed alternative to a request. One of the four acceptable responses to a request.

Declaration: A statement of your commitment.

Fact: Information collectively agreed upon as objectively true.

Fiction: Information you made up; your interpretation. We often mistake our interpretations, such as "my staff is lazy," for being factual and thereby limit possibilities.

Gap: The difference between where things stand now and where you would like them to be. Two key questions: Where are you now? What would you like to have happen?

Integrity: The state of being whole and complete. The two levels of integrity discussed include (1) being true to your word (doing what you say you are going to do) and (2) being true to yourself (acting consistent with your values).

Perspective: The "lenses" or filter through which you are observing a situation. Your perspective on facts determines your interpretation of them (the "fiction" you make up about them).

Promise: A declaration that one will do or refrain from doing something within a stated time frame.
   ◆ A promise has a *who*, a *what*, and a *by when*. "I will do X by Y."
   ◆ Lack of clarity in the making and fulfilling of promises is one of the most common sources of breakdowns, upsets and lack of trust in organizations.
   ◆ Your personal reputation and the reputation of your organization depend on your ability to make and fulfill promises.

Re-negotiate: A conversation to alter a promise before it is due. If you know you will not fulfill a promise you made, contact the promisee and re-negotiate. The sooner you do this the better it will be for your performance, trust and personal power.

Request: The act of asking for a promise.
- A request includes four elements:
  Saying exactly <u>what</u> you want, <u>who</u> you want it from, <u>when</u> you want it, and <u>why</u>.
- Only accept one of these four responses:
  1. Yes (now it's time for a promise!)
  2. No
  3. Counter offer: A proposed alternative to a request.
  4. Commit to respond at a future time
- Any other response will almost certainly result in negative consequences for the task, the relation ship between the two parties, and the personal power of the parties involved.

Trust: Certainty based on past experience. A lack of fear. The greater the trust, the closer you perform to your potential.

Book Creation Acknowledgements

It is humbling to step back and really look at how many people contributed to the creation of this book, and yet see only our names listed as authors. At the risk of missing several people, we take this opportunity to offer a wholehearted **THANK YOU** to:

Ivy Gilbert, Jim Vigue, and Alice Anderson of Power Publications in Longwood, Florida, for all your wonderful writing, editing, and production support and advise; and also for your patience while we re-negotiated our timeline promises. *(If anyone reading this has a book inside of you that you'd like to bring to life, contact Power Publications at www.PeakPowerMarketing.com);*

Nova Berkshires of Sapphire Communications, Inc. for your extensive, expert editing on several versions of this book - you greatly exceeded our expectations each time;

Melinda Hsu for your delightful scripting ideas throughout the process;

Kim D'Angelo and the staff at Bookcovers.com for your excellent design work;

Each of the following people for your ideas, feedback, coaching and mentoring throughout the process: Sean Brawley, Billy Strean, Gayle Van Gils, Tom Jordan, Bill Hoge, Peter Illig, Laurie Berger, Jim Hanson, Andrea Masciana, Dania Douglas, Jay Kamin, Jim Thomas, Mark Fitzgerald, Sandra Crowe, Eileen Hanson, Jay Jamrog, Monica Pipoli, the RP Team at TECO, Joanne Hebert, Charley Thurman, Mark Sierra, Bobby Stark, and Bob Crockett.

And a special thank you to our parents and family for your powerful support throughout this and all other events in our lives.

Book Content
Acknowledgements

We are grateful to the countless people and programs that have influenced us throughout our careers. Your work has become part of us and better enables us to contribute to the lives of others. For this book we particularly express our gratitude to:

Julio Olalla and the Newfield Network coach training program for introducing us formally to the "speech acts" that form the foundation of the Integrity Tools, and more importantly, for introducing us to each other!;

Fred Kofman at Axialent, Inc, along with Richie Gil and Patrick Campiani, for significantly deepening our understanding of "commitment conversations," and introducing us to distinctions such as "victim/player," the three levels affected by integrity, and the success and satisfaction formulas (see their book <u>Metamanagement</u>);

Tim Gallwey for his awareness building coaching practices (e.g., noticing your experience instead of trying to fix or change something) (see <u>Inner Game of Work</u>);

Coaches Training Institute for helping us learn to co-create our coaching relationships;

Flip Flippen of the Flippen Group for his teachings on leadership (e.g., no organization can outperform the constraints of its leadership);

Maria Nemeth for her circle drawings of integrity in her book, The Energy of Money;

Nathanial Brandon for his teachings on self-esteem (e.g., the reputation you have with yourself) (see How To Raise Your Self-Esteem);

Byron Katie for The Work she does transforming lives (see her book Loving What Is);

Jim Collins for his studies of the relationship between employees and their bosses (see Good To Great);

Landmark Education for their commitment to integrity and choosing the lenses through which we see the world;

Spencer Johnson, Ken Blanchard, Richard Bach, E.M. Goldratt, Patrick Lencioni, and Steve Lundin for inspiring the fictional style of our writing;

We admire and recommend the work of all of the people listed above.

About The Authors

Tom Hanson, Ph.D.

CEO of Heads-Up Performance, Inc., Tom is a certified professional coach with 17 years experience coaching, speaking and training. He has a doctorate in sport psychology from the University of Virginia and uses his expertise in human performance to evoke excellence in professional athletes, CEOs and other corporate performers. Formerly a tenured professor at Skidmore College (NY), Hanson co-authored the book *Heads-up Baseball: Playing the Game One Pitch at a Time*, which has sold more than 55,000 copies worldwide. His website, **www.FocusedBaseball.com**, is a "Mental Toughness Resource for Players, Coaches and Parents."

Birgit Zacher Hanson, M.S.,C.P.C.C.

Birgit, president of Heads-Up Performance, Inc., holds a Masters Degree in Applied Behavioral Science from Johns Hopkins University and obtained her coach certificate from the Coaches Training Institute in San Rafael, CA. She has 15 years of international corporate experience, including not for profit organizations, and has a passion for diversity and change management. An accomplished speaker and trainer (who can deliver in several different languages), Birgit is also a sales coach who teaches business owners and sales professionals to use "power tools" that work in today's economy.

Made in the USA
Las Vegas, NV
07 April 2023

70321907R00115